ONE STEP AT A TIME

One Step at a Time

DAVID WAITE

KINGSWAY PUBLICATIONS
EASTBOURNE

Biblical quotations are from the
New International Version © International Bible Society
1973, 1978, 1984.

Cover design by W James Hammond
Back cover photograph by Clint Randall

British Library Cataloguing in Publication Data

Waite, David
One step at a time
1. Church of England. Waite, Terry,
1939–
I. Title
283'.092'4

ISBN 0-86065-706-X

Printed in Great Britain for
KINGSWAY PUBLICATIONS LTD
1 St Anne's Road, Eastbourne, E Sussex BN21 3UN by
Richard Clay Ltd, Bungay, Suffolk
Typeset by Nuprint Ltd, Harpenden, Herts AL5 4SE.

Dedicated to
Daniel, Michael, Caroline and Matthew

Contents

Foreword by the
Archbishop of Canterbury

My first meeting with David Waite took place amidst the shock and uncertainty of Terry's disappearance. I was struck then by David's hopefulness and this, together with his remarkable patience, has continued to impress me during all the months of waiting. I firmly believe that these qualities are products of the strong and simple faith which encounters us on every page of this book.

In telling the story of his life, David describes his spiritual growth as well as his courageous fight against physical disability. As we follow his experiences, 'one step at a time', we begin to understand that, for David, this latest trial is but one of many events which have taught him to gain 'a greater understanding of God's love and care for those who put their trust in him'.

David's story is one which encompasses both the everyday and the miraculous; and both are narrated with that same serene acceptance which characterises the man himself. It may be that some will find it difficult to accept every aspect of David's witness with the same ease; every individual has to find his or her own path to faith, and these paths are as various as the avenues of the human character. What I do know is that there will be few who remain unmoved by his witness. I am grateful to David for writing this book, and I hope that it will lead many to appreciate those qualities of simple faith and trust in God which I so much admire in him.

Robert Contons

Acknowledgements

I wish to thank the following people who made this book possible:

My mother who went through so much to bring me into the world and whose love and friendship I value greatly.

My wife Alison for her help in planning the format of the book, and for her advice and prayers throughout the project.

John and Elizabeth Sherrill, who originally suggested that I write the story of my experiences.

The Archbishop of Canterbury, Dr Robert Runcie, whose help and support throughout the last two years to the Waite family has been greatly appreciated.

Dave Richardson, for his generosity in loaning me his house each day where I could write in peace and quiet away from any distractions.

Eric Atkins for the front cover photograph.

And finally to the many friends both past and present, some of whom are mentioned in this book, whose friendships have enriched my life, each one playing a part in God's overall plan and purpose.

Preface

I don't need to tell you that life is uncertain. On any day of our lives there are so many unknown quantities that literally 'anything can happen'. Some people like life to be unpredictable and haphazard, and that's fine; but others prefer things to be planned and structured, and for those people uncertainties bring stress and tension. People who rely for their security on things like money, health, career or relationships are especially at risk in this way. These things can so easily slip through their fingers, or fail, leaving them disillusioned, and more uncertain than ever.

For those of us within the Body of Christ, our lives can seem equally uncertain, if we are not careful to walk close to the Lord. We too have bills to pay, bodies to care for and relationships to tend. In addition, many Christians seem to have forgotten the wonderful truth that Jesus loves and approves of them, and wants to intervene in their lives.

The good news for the Christian is that he does not have to live his life relying on his own resources: he can make use of the gifts that God had made available to his church— with remarkable results! Then the saying 'anything can happen' takes on an exciting new meaning.

1

Waiting, Hoping and Praying

I am the brother of missing church envoy Terry Waite. As I write this his whereabouts are unknown, his fate uncertain. Over the months that have passed since his disappearance, many people have asked, 'How do you cope with a situation like this?' and 'How have you managed to maintain a positive attitude all this time?'

What they don't realise is that for me, this is only the latest in a series of difficult situations, and through such experiences I have gained a greater understanding of God's love and care for those who put their trust in him. It is this understanding I hope to share through this book.

Ever since Terry disappeared, the press and public interest has been immense. Every twist and turn in the saga has been faithfully reported by the media; sadly, what they have not known they have too often been willing to speculate upon. For the first few months this interest was focused upon Frances, Terry's wife, and Lena, my mother. I watched with horror as some of the press became more and more intrusive in their efforts to get a personal angle on the story.

Terry and Frances live in a tall house in London, and their front door is only a few feet away from the pavement. Reporters would camp outside the house waiting for someone to come out, or try to take photographs of the family through the windows. One or two shouted through the letterbox or followed members of the family when they exercised the dog.

Meanwhile my mother was receiving similar treatment at her home in Cheshire: at one time the police set up a roadblock in an attempt to stop the more irresponsible members of the press from bothering her.

All this was happening during the early months after Terry's disappearance, while we were still trying to make a difficult adjustment. Terry had been very active in trying to arrange the release of Western hostages: now he was a hostage himself.

To relieve the pressure on Frances and my mother, my cousin John took on the role of family spokesman, and managed the press admirably. Things might have gone on like this were it not for a conversation my son Daniel had with a school friend.

The boys were chatting on the way home from school one day when some new rumour had been in the news; Daniel simply remarked to Dominic that Terry Waite was his uncle. Dominic's family thought he was joking when he repeated this at home. It was only a few days later when Dominic's mum met my wife and told her the funny story that they discovered it was true.

Dominic's dad is a reporter for our local radio station, Radio Oxford, and he asked me to do a five-minute interview with him about Terry, and how the family were coping. The interview was picked up by the national network of the BBC and before long we were visited by both BBC Television News, and their rivals at ITN.

I don't think I'll ever forget the first time the BBC News team came to our house. I can't recall which particular incident they wanted to cover, but it was late at night when they first rang us. It would take a little time to get a camera crew together, they said, and to reach our house from London, but would we mind if they came anyway? We wanted to help if we could, and to say something positive, so we agreed, and waited for them to arrive—and waited— and waited! Our part of Oxfordshire was unfamiliar to them all, and they finally arrived on our doorstep at three am, full of apologies! We very much wanted to look calmly optimistic for this interview, but probably ended up looking like victims of insomnia.

This was, incidentally, an isolated incident, and the press and TV companies have been courteous to my family in all the dealings we've had with them.

As each rumour starts, so our telephone springs into life. I've lost count of the number of interviews I've had with the press, and TV appearances are now part of my life. I try whenever possible to introduce my Christian faith into the conversation: I think it's important that people should know who sustains our family.

At first, I admit, we felt as though we were on an emotional rollercoaster. A rumour would surface (often carried by some minor Arab newspaper, quoting no names or sources), for instance, that Terry had had a massive heart attack; that he was dead; that he had been spotted in the Bekar Valley. Immediately the telephone would start to ring, with people asking if we had access to further information, whether it was true, and how we felt.

In fact I very seldom had any extra information, and anything I did know I kept to myself: I didn't intend to start breaking confidences. Neither did I contact Frances—I knew she wouldn't speak to the press, so I preferred not to know her views, so that I couldn't end up doing a sort of interview by proxy for her.

Most of the rumours we discounted at once: there is no history of heart trouble in our family, and Terry has always been physically very fit, so we ignored the suggestion of a heart attack. We do not believe that he is dead. Lambeth Palace have their own contacts in the area, and they all suggest that he is alive and well. In addition, I pray daily for his safety and always feel a deep peace in my heart for him; sometimes I have felt that he has had a particularly tough day, but never once have I or any of the family felt that he was dead.

Some rumours are quite obviously the products of a reporter's vivid imagination, like the story that Terry had renounced his Christian faith and was now an Islamic mullah in Iran. As Terry has been connected with the Anglican Church since he was about four years old, that didn't seem too likely to us, somehow!

On the whole, though, the media have behaved responsibly, avoiding intruding too much on our lives. Because of their initial problems, Frances and my mother have not been involved at all, and since that time the media have taken care not to bother them. I think all the family have shown amazing courage and faith, and I feel sure Terry will be proud of them when he returns.

There is a seven-year age gap between me and Terry, so as children we didn't play together a lot. He always seemed to be off on his bike somewhere, and I couldn't keep up, so I played more with my sister Diana. However, he was always fun to be with when we did spend time together. I can remember going with him on a train ride to Manchester, our nearest large town: he made every mile exciting as he pointed out things of interest along the way, or discussed what we would do when we arrived, or told me about one of his bike rides. Looking back, I can see that it wasn't what we did that was specially exciting, but the zest for life that Terry had, his interest in everything around him.

I was ten when Terry left home in 1956; he travelled a great deal until he returned to settle in London in 1978, and even then he was often on the move for up to ten months of the year. It was a way of life he loved: he has always been the adventurous member of the family, while I have never had the urge to travel at all.

After living so long apart, with neither of us very good at writing letters, I suppose we should have drifted apart. In a way our relationship was 'on hold' for much of that time. Yet even when he was abroad, Terry was always the first person I turned to for help or advice, and he always responded.

His disappearance has underlined for me an important lesson: it is too easy to take family members for granted, and I am saddened that we didn't keep in touch more closely.

Throughout this difficult time we have all received a great deal of support and encouragement from the general public. People do care and they want us to know it: between us we have received hundreds of cards and letters. Prayer groups have written to say they are praying for us, schoolchildren have sent drawings and poems, and complete strangers have rung us to pass on their best wishes.

Until April 1988 I worked as the manager of a painting and decorating shop in Witney, and much of my time was spent in talking to the customers who called to ask if there was any news, or comment on what was happening. I found this both encouraging and tiring: it was good to be aware of people's concern, but wearing to have the same conversation half a dozen times a day. My two shop assistants were on occasion very protective in this respect, and one of them would, I am sure, have taken on the whole

BBC single-handed if she had thought they were taking advantage of me!

It sounds callous, but life goes on, no matter how difficult your circumstances. A friend remarked to me recently that when her father died, it had such a huge effect on her life that she expected everyone else to be affected in some way, too. Of course, that doesn't happen. The birds keep on singing, the sun keeps on shining, people go off on holiday—there's no reason why they shouldn't, but it seems strange when you are dealing with something of overwhelming importance in your own life.

One incident which happened to me was first alarming, then funny, and finally debilitating.

It was a grey day in January 1988. I had a day off from the shop, which was good because I could spend time with my wife Alison and the four children when they came home from school, and also pray about Terry's situation and deal with answering the mail.

However, I woke feeling tired, and as the day dragged on I felt more and more weary. The children watched TV with us for a while after supper, and then I had a bedtime story and prayer time with Caroline and Matthew, the two youngest. As usual, they mentioned Uncle Terry in their prayers. An hour or two later Daniel and Michael went to bed, too, and Ali and I settled down for a few quiet moments together.

Suddenly I had a twinge of pain in my right side. It grew more and more uncomfortable until after only a few minutes I had violent pains in my back.

I am usually very unwilling to take pain killers or visit the doctor, but this was different.

'Ali,' I gasped, 'please get the doctor—quickly!' I was sweating and writhing in agony, and Ali phoned the doctor anxiously. The pain became more acute and Ali looked on

18

helplessly, praying for the doctor to come quickly or for the pain to go away.

When at last the doctor arrived she immediately diagnosed a kidney stone, gave me some painkillers, and said that she would ring us in an hour to see if I was any better. If not, I would have to be admitted to hospital.

Sure enough, in an hour the pain was even worse, so an ambulance was called to take me to the John Radcliffe Hospital in Oxford.

I was seen by a doctor, given some more powerful painkillers and put in a small room where I eventually fell asleep. I was allowed home the next day, and told that if I drank enough water the stone would be expelled naturally, as it was only a small one. (If that was a small one, I never want to have a big one!)

All this happened just before the first anniversary of Terry's disappearance, and so public awareness was high. When the ambulance men announced the arrival of Mr Waite, somehow word got round that it was Terry, flown back unexpectedly and needing treatment. Every so often people would look in on me, and I suppose they were very disappointed to find that it was only me! However, it quickly became known that I was Terry's brother, and amazingly, people came up to me while I was still rolling around on the bed in severe pain, and said, 'Sorry to bother you at the moment, but is there any news about your brother?'

It sounds funny now, but at the time I just wanted to tell them to go away. Even that, though, was a reminder how much people in this country care about Terry and his fate, and at least I was in a pleasant hospital with professional staff to look after me. What conditions Terry and the others have had to endure can only be guessed at.

2

Putting in an Appearance

As we approached the first anniversary of Terry's disappearance in the Lebanon, I was contacted by various newspapers and TV channels, asking if I would contribute in some way to the coverage they planned for that day. Eager to put forward a Christian view of the first year, I willingly agreed. The Archbishop of Canterbury had also planned a special service for Terry to be broadcast live on Radio 4 that day. My mother and sister were unable to travel to London in time, but I was happy to accept the invitation to attend.

My first appointment that day was at *TV-am*, the early morning magazine programme. The staff there kindly arranged transport for me and also overnight accommodation in London. However, I always find it impossible to sleep properly the first night away from home, and so I tossed and turned for hours—the worst possible thing when you know that next morning you will be interviewed live on TV.

To make matters worse, I knew I was going to be interviewed by Anne Diamond for the first time: I had watched her on TV before, and knew that she would really lay into a politician if she thought there was good reason. In any case I generally find the studio atmosphere daunting, with all the lights, cameras and sound systems around.

Before I go on TV I usually ring up a few friends and ask them to pray for me. When I know I am supported in prayer, I can relax and say what I feel is relevant. On this occasion I was concerned about what questions I would be asked, and whether I would be able to answer them intelligently. Suddenly the thought came into my mind: 'Why not ask God what the questions are to be?' It sounded odd at first, but the more I thought about it the better I liked the idea. After all, he knows all things.

I lay quietly in the darkness of my hotel room and asked the Lord to tell me what questions would be asked. After a few minutes the first question formed in my mind. 'What was it like spending Christmas without Terry?' Then, 'Does your faith help to bind you together?' 'How do you react to rumours?' Then another and another. My tension disappeared, and after some time I drifted peacefully off to sleep, thinking that at least I had some idea of what might happen the next day.

When the interview began the following morning I quickly realised that I had no cause to be nervous, as Anne and all the other presenters were charming. In addition, not only were their questions the same ones I had been given the night before, they were even in the same order!

After the interview I had a hearty breakfast in the *TV-am* canteen overlooking Camden Lock, and went out to find the car they had arranged to take me to Lambeth Palace. However, neither I nor the transport office at *TV-am* had reckoned on the extraordinary amount of traffic in London that day. As the minutes ticked by and we crawled along the busy roads, I realised there was very little chance that I would arrive in time for the start of the service at ten forty-five. The driver did everything he could to help, rushing down side streets, taking strange short cuts and breaking one or two rules of the highway code, while I sat silently praying in the back seat!

At last Lambeth Palace came into view, but a new problem loomed. The huge wooden doors of the palace were beseiged by an army of press photographers: word had leaked out that Frances would be attending the service. Fortunately the staff at the palace had arranged for her to use another entrance, so the pressmen missed her, but here was someone else for them to photograph—me! I managed to get to the bell, and pulled as hard as I could, hoping the doorman wouldn't think it was the whole of Fleet Street ringing it. He opened the door quickly, and I dived inside, dumped my suitcase at his feet and ran as fast as I could to where the service was being held in the crypt.

I collapsed into my seat thirty seconds before the service went on the air.

The Archbishop chose his words carefully, and managed to express something of what we were all feeling that day— care, concern, sorrow, and trust in God. As we sang the hymns there in the crypt, one of the oldest rooms in London, I was aware more than ever of the agelessness of God and his care and protection for us wherever we are.

Prayers were said for the other British hostages, John McCarthy and Brian Keenan, and I was glad to see that Jill Morrell was also present. I chatted to her after the service and was interested to hear her views, for her stance has been different from our own. She has been tireless in putting pressure on the government to act, and in keeping her boyfriend John McCarthy in the public eye. We, on the other hand, have acted very little, being confident that everything possible has been done by both the government and the church.

After a hasty cup of coffee with some of the guests at the service, I travelled to another studio in London to be interviewed for an American breakfast-time programme. This was 'Good Morning America', hosted by Barbara Walters, one of the highest-paid interviewers in the United States, and not a lady to cross, I gathered.

First I recorded an interview to be used later in the day, in which I spoke to Charles Glass, who had himself been held as a hostage. Then I sat in front of a camera to speak to Barbara Walters and Peggy Say, the sister of Terry Anderson, an American hostage. I was pleased to find that Peggy was a Christian, and that we had each been praying for the other's situation.

It wasn't easy to concentrate during that interview: for one thing, although they could see me, I could only hear them, and it was rather like holding a telephone conversation with someone several thousand miles away. The other problem was my awareness of the time: I had to travel across London yet again to join ITN for the lunchtime news, which was on the air at twelve thirty. At twelve fifteen we had only just started talking, and I knew the traffic was going to hold me up.

After a few questions I heard Barbara say,

'We'll leave it right there and we'll be back in a few moments.'

She then explained that the broadcast had stopped for a commercial break, and that she wanted to ask me a few further questions.

'I'm very sorry,' I replied, 'but I have to leave immediately to get to another studio.'

Charles Glass was still sitting with me, and he put in,

'David, that's fine—if you have to go, just go!' I unclipped the microphone and took out the earpiece they had equipped me with, and hurried away. As I reached the door one of the technicians stopped me and asked what was happening.

'Barbara Walters wanted to ask me a few more questions,' I replied, 'but I said no.'

The colour drained from his face.

'But nobody ever says no to Barbara Walters!' he protested.

'Well, I just did,' I said, and dashed off to get in the lift.

Downstairs a driver was waiting to take me to ITN, and we set off at a snail's pace into the London traffic. The car was fitted with a telephone, and every few minutes the studio staff rang to ask our position—usually only a few yards further on from the previous call.

In the end the driver turned to me and suggested that I abandon the car and walk, as we'd never get through the traffic in time. He pointed me in the general direction of the studio, and off I ran while he parked the car. By now the rain was coming down heavily and I was beginning to wonder whether it was really worth all this effort, when I spotted a young man in shirtsleeves running towards me— he was the search party! We set off down the street at a rapid pace, the ITN man in front, me in second place, and the driver puffing and panting behind.

We arrived in the newsroom with seconds to spare, and I shall never know how I managed to have a relaxed and positive interview. I'm sure Julia Somerville, the newsreader, had no idea of the chaos preceding my arrival.

It was an amazing day; my concern about Terry, sharpened by the anniversary, was overlaid with all the pressures and anxieties of the tight schedule of TV appearances. Yet through it all I had great peace, and could see the humour of my various predicaments.

During the first year or so of Terry's absence, I was still working at the decorating shop I managed. I made some very good friends in the eight years I was there, and enjoyed the daily banter with the customers. Witney is a lovely market town in the heart of Oxfordshire, and there seems to be a strong Christian witness there: most of the churches have good attendances, and I have always found it a very caring place.

Most of our customers were the ordinary folk of the town, but occasionally we saw a famous face or two—such as John Patten and Douglas Hurd, both local MPs. Another person I saw regularly was Dr Graham Leonard, the Bishop of London. He sometimes dropped in to have a chat about Terry's situation, but quite often we ended up discussing varnish or brushes or something.

I remember one day when I was specially busy: the shop badly needed tidying up, and I had masses of paperwork to complete and send to our head office. I decided to leave the muddle of wallpaper, pots of paint and cardboard boxes, while I sorted out the mountain of forms and invoices.

I was working at the counter, surrounded by paper, when I heard a car turning into the side entrance. Glancing up, I caught sight of the profile of the Bishop of London in the rear; I was cross that I hadn't tidied up, but I knew he wouldn't mind. I waited for him to come in, but heard instead a knock at the rear door of the shop, and a muffled conversation. I turned round to see, picking his way across the shop floor, the Archbishop of Canterbury! I was so surprised to see him that I couldn't at all remember the correct form of address, and just jumped off my stool and said, 'Hi, how are you?' Dr Leonard introduced us, and we chatted for a while about Terry and the current situation. I found him to be warm and friendly and very approachable. I am sure that history will remember him as a man who initiated many things, and who refused to accept the status quo.

I can't speak too highly of the way Lambeth Palace have looked after us as a family. Before Terry's disappearance I had had no contact with the Archbishop, Dr Runcie, or his staff. For a while at first we thought Terry might just have gone into hiding to escape the press, but when it became clear that he had been taken hostage, Lambeth Palace at once contacted us and gave us all the information they had at the time. Since then they have been in touch constantly, reassuring us when rumours are circulated, responding with help and advice when it is needed, and dealing with this very difficult situation in a most compassionate and professional way.

Terry's absence means that his workload has to be carried by others, and the circumstances of his disappearance create even more work. Two officials in particular, Mrs Eve Keatley and Mr John Lyttle, have been wonderful to us—not just by keeping us fully informed, but by remembering birthdays and anniversaries, sending flowers to Frances and my mother, and generally acting in a loving and caring manner. I have often been annoyed when people say 'Shouldn't Lambeth Palace be doing more?' The Archbishop and his staff have worked tirelessly for Terry's release along with the other hostages, and when he returns, as I am sure he will, it will be largely due to their efforts.

As I write this we still don't know the ultimate outcome, but I am sure the whole situation is in God's hands. Meanwhile, I'd like to tell you the rest of my story—and how God prepared me for living with uncertainty.

3

Family Life

At the time I was born, my parents were living in a small Cheshire village called Styal. Styal was one of those lovely, sleepy villages in England where nothing much ever happened, and everyone knew everyone else. My father was the village 'bobby', and we lived in the Police House, a pleasant red-brick building with a large front garden. By the gate was a board saying 'Cheshire County Constabulary', where notices were posted about outbreaks of foot-and-mouth disease, or the need to look out for Colorado Beetle, or the odd 'missing' or 'wanted' sign. The back garden was even bigger, with a large lawn, and beyond it Dad's vegetable garden and fruit trees. The police wage wasn't very high, so we really appreciated Dad's potatoes, lettuce, raspberries, blackcurrants and strawberries. People who have never enjoyed home-grown produce won't know what I mean, but the taste of newly pulled potatoes from the garden is something quite special.

Dad was a tall thin man, very devoted to his duty; often a planned family outing was cancelled because of some emergency or other. He was dedicated to his job, and won several medals for bravery. It wasn't his way to get as many convictions as possible, but rather to have a gentle word with offenders—or sometimes, in the case of tough young lads from Manchester who thought they were smart, a not-so-gentle word. His bark was worse than his bite, however, and he was essentially very shy and quiet. A highly intelligent man, he was skilled with both words and figures, and could turn his hand to anything from dress designing to woodwork.

Sometimes his methods of dealing with offenders were unconventional—like the time he had to escort several youths from Wilmslow to Styal. There were too many of them for him to handle adequately, so before they boarded the train he removed all their belts: the only way to keep their trousers up was to keep their hands in their pockets, which hampered them sufficiently to make escape impossible!

Once he brought home a man who had tried to commit suicide in the Styal woods; he sat him down in a deckchair on the lawn with a glass of brandy, before trying to sort out his problems. Dad was remembered for a long time in Styal as a wonderful policeman of the old school.

Inside the house Mum was always busy, with a growing family to feed and clothe. Before she married, Mum had been a confectioner, so as well as baking all our own bread and cakes, she often made Christmas and wedding cakes for people in the village.

Our lives had a small compass in those early years: there was a Post Office down the road, where we bought ice creams in summer and sat under the huge tree outside to eat them. Around it was a cluster of shops—a butcher, a shoe-repairer, a pub with a hall upstairs where confirmation classes were held—and we knew all the shopkeepers and they knew us. Styal village was a caring and concerned community, and a wonderfully secure environment in which to grow up.

Because of Dad's job, ours was a mobile family: Terry was born in Bollington where my parents lived for a while after their marriage: then they moved to Hembrey where Diana was born, and then to Styal where I arrived.

My arrival was a time of uncertainty in itself, since it was unplanned. One Saturday two months before the birth was due, my mother took Terry and Diana into Wilmslow, the nearest large town, to shop. As Diana was only four, they took the pushchair which had to be put in the guard's van on the train. While Mum was doing this, the guard accidentally slammed a door shut on her hand. The pain of this made her feel ill, and so she stopped for a while at a friend's house and then returned home. The shock must have been greater than she thought, for that night she realised that she had gone into labour.

She woke Dad, who went downstairs to telephone for the doctor; when he returned he found that I had already been born, and Mum was unconscious.

I weighed a pathetic two and a half pounds: when the doctor arrived he said there was not much chance that I would survive the day. Like many people in those days, Mum believed that if a child died unbaptised its soul would not go to heaven, so it was very important to her that this scrap of humanity should be christened forthwith. That Sunday afternoon, the Rector was called out to officiate. There was an unexpected delay when his car refused to start, and Mum and Dad waited anxiously, willing their tiny baby to hang on to life until it could be baptised. They were immensely relieved when the Rector finally arrived.

Now a new problem presented itself—what to call the infant? Mum and Dad hadn't even got round to choosing names yet, and it didn't seem to matter too much, since I wasn't likely to be around for long. Still, a name had to be chosen.

Enter Terry, fresh from Sunday School. Terry always had a mind of his own, and had insisted on going to Sunday School ever since he was four. Usually Mum took him, or if Dad was working and she couldn't leave Diana, an old man from the next village would call for him. On one notable occasion Terry had waited as usual by the gate for his elderly escort, but the old man didn't turn up. As the church bells had started ringing, Terry simply went on alone. He sat through the service by himself and came home afterwards unaccompanied. Mum was horrified at what might have happened, but pleased that church meant so much to him.

As the family discussed various names, Terry announced that his Sunday School lesson that day had been about David and Jonathan, the shepherd lad and the prince who became firm friends. Why not call the baby David, or Jonathan—or David John? The names seemed as good as any, so I was duly christened there in my parents' bedroom, on the day I was born.

I have always been grateful to that unknown teacher who chose the story of David and Jonathan for Terry and his classmates that day, rather than the story of David and the Philistine giant. It would have been trying to go through life as David Goliath Waite!

One tinge of sadness overshadowed the simple ceremony. Only Dad and the doctor knew that with me there had been a stillborn twin. Mum had always wanted four children, but because of the trauma of the birth Dad did not tell her of the other child until some time later. We three children were not told for many years, and that, I think, caused me some problems later on. Meanwhile, Mum and Dad had a hard task on their hands just keeping me alive.

It was 1946, and the country was still recovering from the war. Rationing was still in force, and many necessities were in short supply. Incubators were virtually unknown, but the doctor said that I had to be kept at a constant temperature, day and night, for the first two months: the only heating in the room was a coal fire. In addition, I had to be fed every two hours with a mixture of breast milk, glucose and brandy! I have no idea how my parents managed. Dad worked shifts at the police station, so there were many sleepless nights for them both. Terry and Diana were sent away to relatives at first, but Diana was back after two days, and Terry after three weeks. Mum decided that however hard the work, it was better for the family if we were all together.

The strain must have been enormous; Mum recalls one night when they were so exhausted that they slept through my usual feed time and woke to find that I was turning blue from lack of nourishment. My delicate skin had to be bathed in olive oil, and when, after three months, I was bathed in water for the first time, they were amazed to see that their dark-haired baby had a shock of blond curls!

As I grew, other problems became apparent. My twin had died in the womb, but the presence of its body had restricted the growth of my own. My right side was weak, and my right leg shorter than the left. I crawled normally, but showed no sign of walking; several specialists saw me and doubted whether I would ever be able to walk.

My parents, however, had put so much effort into raising me that they weren't going to give up without a fight. At last they found a specialist who agreed that there might be a chance that I would walk, but first my legs must get stronger. The heavier my body became, the less chance my wasted legs would have of carrying me.

Dad, always an innovator, had an idea. He took two of our dining chairs, removed the seats, and put castors on the legs; then he plonked me in one and my sister in the other (for company) and told us we could play trams up and down the hallway. I guess he invented the world's first babywalker. I loved it, and we zoomed up and down having fun, while exercising my legs. There was, however, no sign of my walking unaided. Diana used to push me around in a pram, though she wasn't strong enough to lift me out: when we went round to the builder's and joiner's yard next door she would just tip the pram up over a pile of sand and let me slide out head first!

Then another drama hit our little family. Mum had to go into hospital for two weeks for an operation. This was quite a big event for a three-year-old to cope with, even with Dad at home to cook the meals. I was overjoyed when Mum came safely home, but when she told me she had to keep an outpatients' appointment at the hospital for a checkup I assumed that she would be gone for another fortnight. So I was surprised, later that afternoon, to see her walk in through the living-room door. As she came in I looked up, and was so amazed to see her that I got up and walked towards her. Mum cried out, 'Look, David's walking!' and no one could believe what was going on. Everyone seemed to be laughing and crying, but I felt a tremendous surge of excitement as I took my first ever steps at the age of three years and one month.

First I walked around the room, then out into the hall where the 'trams' were parked. Then I went into the pantry to gaze at the rows of jars of home-made jam, then into Dad's study, where he interviewed all the naughty boys caught scrumping apples. I could walk on my own—I was independent at last.

The thoughts racing through my brain were just as unusual as what was happening to my legs. Ours was a family where the name of Christ was hardly ever mentioned, and spiritual things were not discussed. But there was one overwhelming thought in my head as I walked around the house for the first time ever: 'There must be a God, if I'm walking at last. There must be a God!' I don't know where the thought came from, to a child so young, but I know it wouldn't go away. There must be a God—but it was to be a few years before I found out for sure.

4

Growing Up

Life took on a new dimension now that I could move around on my own: no longer did I have to wait for my Mum to come along to carry me where I wanted to go. The 'trams' were used less and less and finally discarded. I didn't walk properly, of course, for my right side was too weak and stunted; my right foot pointed inwards, and because my legs were different lengths, my right heel did not touch the ground.

However, I quickly adapted to this rather lumbering way of walking, and it was such fun to be able to get around unaided that I was blissfully unaware that I was any different from anyone else. Mum and Dad had the good sense to treat me exactly like the other two children, which was the best possible attitude.

I appreciated my new freedom. Before I could walk I spent most of my time at home with Mum while she did the housework: I especially remember her doing the washing on Mondays, with clouds of steam coming from the dolly tub. Later in the week she would do the ironing, surrounded by that peculiar warm damp smell, while she listened to Concert Hour on the Home Service of the BBC.

Now I was released from the house, and could spend those afternoons out in the garden, or playing at a friend's house. I must have hated the restrictions of those early days, because for many years the two things I associated with them—the smell of ironing, and classical music—filled me with a profound feeling of depression.

It quickly became clear that although I was now walking I still needed some kind of transport to help me get around. Home-made 'trams' were all right indoors, but now I was getting older and more independent, I needed something more conventional.

A tricycle was the answer, and my parents took me to Manchester, 'Just looking,' they said. I quickly spotted one that was like something out of a dream! It was painted a shiny post-box red, with a little straw basket at the front (useful for putting conkers in, I thought) and what can only be described as a boot at the back. My parents ordered it, although warily, they didn't tell me what they had done.

However, only a few days later Dad met someone who lived on the outskirts of the village who had a second-hand tricycle for sale. It seemed a good idea to save so much money, and the bike was brought to our house. Quite a lot of paint had chipped off it, the bell was rusty, and there was no 'boot' at the back—but it was a bike and it would enable me to get around faster.

Everything would have been all right, if the shop hadn't delivered the first tricycle by accident. A huge delivery van stopped outside our house, and the driver said cheerily,

'Hallo, sonny, I think we've got something for you!'

My parents came running down the path.

'No, that's not for us,' called my mother, 'we've cancelled it.'

But it was too late—I had glimpsed the red bike in the back, waiting to be unloaded. I began to howl with disappointment, and the man shut the van again, looking confused and embarrassed. My parents tried to explain, but I didn't want to be reasoned with. Of course they were right, and I'm sure that in their situation I would have done exactly the same thing. However, it was the first time I can remember feeling disappointment so acute it ached.

My friend Alan and I had great fun on our bikes, racing from our house to the Post Office on the corner. The trick was to get in the lead going down the front garden path from the house: if you were in front then, the race was usually yours. On at least one occasion I ran straight into an innocent pedestrian who happened to be passing the police house at the wrong moment.

'Steady on, or I'll tell your Dad,' I was told—an ever-present threat when your Dad was the local policeman.

Occasionally the whole family would be invited to Mr Renshaw's for tea. 'Uncle Tom' was a favourite with us (though no relation). He had no children, and lived with his wife, Mary, her sister and a housekeeper. I think he may have felt a little outnumbered, for he would often come to his joinery business next door to our house, even on a Sunday.

He would hammer away on one of the workbenches to let us know he had arrived, and we would yell, 'Mr Renshaw's there!' and dash round to see what he was doing. We knew we were always welcome. He made toys for us—wooden stilts and swords—and seemed to enjoy our chattering company. He allocated each of us a box of nails, and would ask us politely before using one of 'our' nails. He was always a tease when we were in his workshop, insisting, for instance, that one of the tools hanging up there was for 'winding the sun up'.

He was a very important figure in our lives—partly, I suppose, because he was around so much of the time, unlike our dad. So often Dad would be either at work, or asleep in bed after a night shift, and we would have to creep around the house for fear of waking him. At Mr Renshaw's, however, we could make as much noise as we liked, and he seemed always to be willing to listen to us and let us play. Terry used to have great fun walking over the rafters above our heads where long planks of wood were stored.

Tea at the Renshaws' was a formal occasion. We were warned to be on our best behaviour, but between the three of us we always managed to do something wrong. Mrs Renshaw wasn't used to children, and served food that appealed to adult tastes rather than children's. The table was covered with a snowy white tablecloth, and the best silverware was brought out. We were offered meat paste or crab sandwiches, followed by seed cake or rice mould for dessert.

The rule was that we mustn't make a fuss about food we didn't like, but eat everything we were given. Mrs Renshaw would say, 'Do have some rice mould, Diana,' and a look of horror would come over Diana's face. She found it difficult to tackle new foods, anyway, but before she could answer Terry would chime in, 'Yes, do have some rice mould, Diana.' He loved to tease her, and furious kicking under the table ensued, as Diana retaliated in the only way available.

When it was time for me to start at the village school, my parents had a word with the teacher. It was agreed that I should be allowed to go to school on my tricycle, but that otherwise I was to be treated just like all the other children. However, a different set of rules applied in the playground, as every child knows.

Nothing had prepared me for my first experience in the playground. A child from another class came up to me and asked,

'Why do you walk like that?'

I didn't know how to answer. To me it was like asking 'Why is your hair fair?' or, 'Why are your eyes blue?' That's just the way things are. Then another kid came along and said,

'Why are you a cripple?' and as he said it he mimicked the way I walked. A little crowd gathered, with other children imitating me, and I stood in the middle of them, helpless and confused. What did 'cripple' mean?

It wasn't the words that hurt—they meant nothing to me at the time—but the spirit in which they were said. I learned then the power of words, to heal or wound. I had committed the greatest crime of the playground: I was different. I started to cry, and more of the children joined in the game which got such an immediate response from their quarry.

I think it was my friend Alan who pulled me out of the crowd and found a teacher to comfort me—but even as my tears were dried I was beginning to realise the truth. I was different, I did have a problem, and there wouldn't always be a friend or a teacher to protect me. I had to learn to deal with it on my own.

The weapon I found was humour—not turned against the aggressor, but against myself. If a child said something nasty to make the others laugh, I would quickly think of something better, and make the 'audience' laugh even louder. It worked well: it made my tormentor's joke sound feeble, and it took all the fun out of it for him if he could see that I wasn't hurt. In the end the kids who started this sort of thing either got fed up with it and went away, or else they got to know me and became friends.

I suppose that the one thing it taught me was not to take myself too seriously. I love meeting people, but still find it difficult to get on with people who are filled with their own importance. However, even when I was telling a joke against myself and laughing with the others, I was aching inside. I longed to be like other people.

Meanwhile the world was changing: at first there was just one TV in the village, and we were sometimes allowed to watch, staring in wonder as the heavy wooden doors of its cabinet opened to reveal a tiny twelve-inch screen. After a while there were several sets around, and Dad bought ours so we could see the broadcast of the coronation of Queen Elizabeth II.

We were fascinated by all the different programmes we could now watch, but my most vivid memory is of an outside broadcast of those early days. The BBC covered a service conducted by the controversial young evangelist from the United States called Dr Billy Graham. He was controversial because he would preach a message and ask people to respond by leaving their seats and walking to the front of the hall to dedicate their lives to Christ.

We tuned in to watch, and to listen to the hymns that were sung with great feeling by the choirs. Then Dr Graham preached his message: I understood it clearly, even though I was only about six at the time. He said that if you trusted Jesus he would forgive all the wrong things you had done. You could make a fresh start and he would help you to live the way God wanted you to. At the end, he said that all those who wanted to dedicate their lives to Jesus should come out to the front.

I wished that I was in the Harringey Stadium that night; although I was so young, I wanted that security he had been talking about. Then he said something that gave me hope.

'And for all you who are watching at home, who can't come out here, I want you to close your eyes, right there in your living-room, if you want to respond to this message tonight.'

This was my chance, and I closed my eyes and waited for the prayer to begin. Suddenly I was aware of giggling beside me. The family thought it was really funny that I was doing what I was told by someone on the TV.

I was embarrassed, and quickly opened my eyes; nevertheless, a seed was planted that night—it just needed a few more years to germinate.

Soon after this we had some news that hit me like a bombshell—we were to leave Styal. Dad had been stationed there for nine years, and it was time to move on. I couldn't believe it: I'd just been accepted by the other kids at school, and now I'd have to start all over again. We had to leave all our friends behind. Mr Renshaw found it very hard: just as we had seen him as a father-figure, so he had regarded us as his adopted children, and our departure was as painful for him as it was for us. He died a few years after we left Styal.

We moved to Thelwall in Cheshire, and I hated it from the moment we arrived. The house was damp, we lived on a busy road, and I didn't like the school. I had to fight all the same battles over again with a different set of kids, and although the teachers were kind, I had a tough time in the classroom too. Some of the teaching methods were very different from those I was used to, and I was utterly confused. It didn't help that Dad was an absolute whizz at maths, and couldn't understand why the light didn't dawn for me. To my annoyance, someone in the school obviously liked concerts, because we always seemed to be rehearsing for a concert or presenting one.

The only good thing about Thelwall as far as I was concerned was that it had the Manchester Ship Canal running through it. There was no bridge, so you crossed the canal in a small rowing boat: the journey there and back cost one old penny, a bargain even in those days. Terry got friendly with the ferryman, and was soon using his own considerable strength to scull people across the canal. The fun was to cross to the other side just after a big liner had gone through, when the wash would make the water turbulent.

Terry loved anything physically demanding and exciting like that, and he always found it easy to strike up an acquaintance with anyone who was doing something he was interested in. He used to go to Ringway Airport to watch the planes, and became friendly with a man who owned a light aircraft. One day he came home and remarked casually that he had flown over our house! Soon this became a regular jaunt, until one day Terry wasn't able to go up as usual. That day the plane crashed and the pilot was killed.

As Terry was always head and shoulders taller than the rest of his gang, he stood out while the others could remain anonymous in the crowd. Consequently if any mischief was afoot, the one person who was always recognised and remembered was Terry. One very snowy winter's day a lady in our street heard her letter-box snap shut. Thinking it was the postman, she went out into the hall, only to find a large snowball dripping on her doormat. She pulled open the front door and looked down the street, just in time to see a crowd of lads disappearing round the corner. Of course, the only one she spotted was Terry, so he was the one who had to go and apologise!

As time went on and I became more independent I sometimes accompanied my big brother on outings, but I never had his love of adventure. I suppose my disability showed up more beside this big towering teenager, but it never bothered me particularly; we were just different, with different interests and activities.

We spent three years at Thelwall, and then moved on again to Lymm, a pretty village between Manchester and Liverpool. This time I settled into a new home and school more easily: I was older and more used to the idea of moving. By this time I was ten, Diana fourteen, and Terry seventeen and an amazing six feet, seven inches tall. He decided to join the Grenadier Guards when he left school: he liked the opportunities for travel an army career would offer. Diana and I were the stay-at-home type, and enjoyed hearing of his travels from the security of our own living-room!

Then Diana joined the commercial course at school, and Dad bought her a typewriter so that she could practise at home. So that I wouldn't feel left out, I suppose, he bought another antiquated typewriter for me to mess around on. I loved it, and started to type out plays (using one finger) for my classmates to perform at school. I suppose all those concerts at Thelwall had got to me at last. However, I soon got fed up with the time it took to type with one finger, so I borrowed Diana's typing book and taught myself to type properly.

Once Diana had found a secretarial job in Warrington, I began to get bored with school and to look forward to getting out into the 'real world' myself. As luck would have it, I didn't have to wait too long. It was my typing that secured me my first job: the town clerk saw some work I did for an open day at school, and offered me a job as office junior at the local council offices.

I enjoyed the change from school life, and the extra independence, and soon settled down at work. It was there I made a new friend, Philip Lofthouse, who worked in the rates department. He was young, full of life, and keen to get on in his job: he used to cycle all the way to work and then have a game of football in the yard before starting work in the morning! He was also a regular churchgoer.

We sometimes had lunch together and became friends—something I appreciated especially. Ever since leaving Styal I had found it hard to settle down: even when surrounded by a crowd of people I often felt lonely. I believe this is a common experience among people who have lost a twin, although at the time I still didn't know about this; it's as though you are missing the person you shared your life with before birth.

Things weren't too good at home, either. Dad had an accident while on duty one night: following up an alarm call from a store in Lymm, he chased the intruder, scaled a wall, and jumped off after him. Unfortunately Dad landed badly and broke a toe. His superior officer decided he was no longer fit for duty, and he had to leave the police force, although he had only eighteen months to serve before retirement. This left him feeling very bitter, and he took legal action against the police authority.

I wasn't any help, caught up in my own feelings of isolation and the usual teenage troubles, and we clashed a lot at home. We were each too absorbed in our own despair and frustration to have any sympathy for the other. Gradually our relationship broke down and in the end we stopped speaking to each other altogether.

When Philip suggested that I might like to go on a holiday he was planning with some friends, I jumped at the chance to get away from home for a while. He warned me that it was going to be a Christian holiday, but I thought that whatever that meant, it couldn't be worse than the atmosphere at home.

The holiday was at Filey, in Yorkshire, at a Butlins Holiday Camp: each year the Movement for Worldwide Evangelisation took over the site for one week at the end of September. Hundreds of people, mainly from the north of England, would assemble to enjoy the holiday facilities of

Butlins in the day time, but instead of bingo and ballroom dancing in the evenings, there would be gospel meetings.

By the time I was due to go on holiday I'd got to know several of the other members of the party. Trevor, a tall, curly-headed chap, was training to be an electrician: he owned a beaten-up old car, and would go miles out of his way giving lifts to his mates who didn't have transport. Jeff, Trevor's cousin, worked as a barber in Warrington. We had great fun together: Trevor had a loud, booming laugh, while Jeff's was almost silent. Whenever I had my hair cut by Jeff, and cracked a joke, the scissors would stop snipping and I would look in the mirror to see what was happening: Jeff would be standing there, helpless with laughter but not making a sound!

We all set off by coach from Warrington. It was the usual scene of people going away for a break: suitcases being piled into the back of the coach, friends waving goodbye. I didn't know many people on the coach, and I wondered whether I was doing the right thing. Once we were under way I had even more doubts: everyone started singing Christian choruses. I was acutely embarrassed by all the singing and hand-clapping, and wondered how adults could behave like that!

Once at the camp I found I was sharing a chalet with Philip, though in the event I didn't see much of him. He went off playing football with friends (something I couldn't join in with), and I spent more time with Trevor and his mates. We had a marvellous time. There was an outdoor and an indoor pool, with glass sides so that people in the adjacent cafe could watch the swimmers underwater, and various coffee bars and snack bars where there was always much laughter and good fun. I began to relax a bit more with these Christians, and realised that they were very much like me—but without a lot of my hangups.

The first evening we went to a meeting in the ballroom. There was more singing, followed by an evangelical message on how to become a Christian. It suddenly reminded me of watching Billy Graham on TV all those years ago. Again I wanted to respond, but I couldn't walk out in front of all those people. What if I found it didn't work, this Christian life, or what if I couldn't stand the pace and became even more disenchanted with life? What if people laughed at me because of the way I walked?

That message made more sense to me than I had ever heard in my life; I wanted so much to make a commitment. I hung on to the underside of my chair: I wanted to resist the temptation to get up, and there was no way I was going to walk to the front without taking the chair with me!

The meeting finally closed, and we all went out to a coffee bar. To my relief, no one talked much about the meeting; most of the lads came from fairly strict Christian homes, and they had probably heard similar messages most of their lives. While I was contemplating coming into the Christian life, I could sense that some of them, at least, were trying to throw off a few restraints.

So the week went on. We had a talk in the morning on Hebrews 11 ('by faith') by David Sheppard—not the famous Anglican bishop, but a wonderful Welsh minister who spoke with conviction and power, yet with such gentleness that his ministry remains with me to this day. The rest of the time was spent going down to the beach, meeting with others for coffee or going to the pool. I felt more relaxed as each day went by, and laughed more than I had for years. I coped with the evening meetings by reasoning that I didn't have to make an immediate decision to become a Christian, and matters like that could wait until I was in a less emotionally-charged atmosphere. It was all a big excuse, of course, for putting off what I knew I should be doing, but I wasn't going to admit that to myself or anyone else!

On the Thursday evening I was late getting ready for the evening meeting, and the others went on ahead. Full of anxiety to get there before it started, I tried to run, and in my clumsy efforts to move quickly, I fell and landed heavily on my arm.

When I finally arrived the hall was almost full, and I had to sit right at the front. As the hymns were sung, my injured arm began to hurt badly, and just as the speaker was about to begin, I decided I couldn't bear the pain any longer.

The speaker was at the microphone, but paused when he saw me get up, and waited as I made my lonely way down the central aisle to the back of the hall. It was quite silent, and I felt as though four thousand pairs of eyes were following me. The back of the hall was mainly glass, and I was so anxious to get out that I panicked, and couldn't tell which panels were doors and which windows. I rattled the handles desperately, and eventually found one which would open. I made my escape, only to be followed by a resounding crash as the door slammed behind me. Everyone knew that I'd walked out of the meeting that night.

5

New Friends

I woke up the next morning feeling sad for the first time since I had arrived. Friday already, and the holiday was almost over. Back to work, back to the situation at home, and back to my loneliness. I tried not to think about the future as I got ready for breakfast, and consoled myself that I did have one more day to go before we headed back to Cheshire.

That afternoon, as I was on my way to the swimming pool, I was stopped by a young man with bright smiling eyes and masses of ginger hair.

'Hi,' he said. 'My name's Dave Bell, but everybody calls me Ding. Aren't you the fellow who walked out of the meeting last night?'

I admitted that I was, but before I could explain why it all happened, he invited me round to his chalet for coffee later on.

When I arrived that evening I chatted to Ding and his girlfriend Jeannette for a while, but the conversation soon got around to Christianity.

'Look,' said Ding, 'I don't need to tell you that you're a sinner—you already know that. What I want to tell you is

47

that God loves sinners and sent his Son Jesus to die for them.'

With Jeannette chiming in every so often, he went on to explain how I could have a real relationship with God, and know that every single sin I had ever committed was forgiven and forgotten. Didn't I want that?

Of course I did. Didn't everyone? My life had been getting into more and more of a mess, with depression and frustration holding sway most of the time. Just being with these Christians had lifted my spirits no end—what would it be like, then, if I actually became a Christian? Could it really work for me?

Just then someone else came into the room, and rather than continue with a conversation that might embarrass me, Ding and Jeannette dropped the subject.

When at last I got back to my chalet I was glad to find that Philip was still out. I needed time to think things out on my own. I felt as though my life was at a crossroads and I had to make a decision. I could choose to do nothing, and let myself be engulfed by the blackness and despair I so often felt—or I could choose to trust in Christ and make a new start: be 'born again' as it said in the Bible.

The more I thought about it the more I realised I didn't really have any choice. The only way open was to submit myself to God, and let him begin to sort out the mess my life had become. I sank onto my knees beside the bed and told the Lord how sorry I was for the things I had done, the way I'd messed things up. I hated my frustration and anger and bad temper and wanted to be rid of them. I knew that I'd hurt people in the past, particularly my Dad: nine months had gone by without us speaking a word to each other.

I asked Jesus to cleanse me from all that sin, and to come into my heart and take control of my life. I didn't see any great light, or hear any heavenly choirs, but I do remember a weight being lifted from deep within me, and a glorious feeling of peace. I felt so full of joy I could shout! But it was the early hours of the morning, so I just quickly got ready for bed and went to sleep.

As soon as I woke the next morning I remembered what I'd done. Did I still feel the same? Yes—that awful weight had lifted and I knew something deep inside had changed. But would it last? How could I be sure I was a Christian? All my old doubts about my ability to live a Christian life came flooding back; I decided not to tell anyone what I'd done. That way, if I did fail, I would be the only one to know.

Soon it was time to pack my suitcase and head for the coach. I tried not to feel despondent about returning home—at least I had someone to help me through it all now, and a new view of life. I could see clearly now how wrong my attitude towards my Dad had been, and I wanted more than anything to put things right with him— a change of heart if ever there was one. Before I went away wild horses wouldn't have dragged me to make the first move.

During the coach trip home I heard some of the lads talking about a meeting they were going to that night, in Manchester. I knew I couldn't join them as I couldn't get there from Lymm, but just then Trevor leaned across to me.

'Do you want to come, Dave? I'll give you a lift if you do.' I accepted eagerly, glad of the chance to see everyone again so soon. Maybe this wasn't the end of the friendships I'd made, after all.

When I got home my Mum took one look at me and said, 'Whatever's happened to you?' Startled, I looked at her. What could she mean? Was it the ultra-short haircut Jeff gave me the night before we left, the string of late nights I had at Filey, the sunburn—or the new faith I'd acquired?

'Where's Dad?' I asked. It was her turn to look startled.

'Why on earth should you want to know that, when you haven't spoken to him for months?' she demanded.

I couldn't explain without giving away my secret, and anyway I wanted to get ready for the meeting that night, so I shrugged and went up to my room.

When we arrived at the Central Hall in Manchester it was just like being back at Filey again. I enjoyed the meeting, and as I was chatting afterwards I spotted a familiar face across the room—Ding! I hadn't expected to see him again. He pushed his way through the crowd to greet me.

'Hi, Dave, good to see you again. Tell me, are you a Christian yet?'

Now I was in a dilemma—I didn't really want anyone to know, but I could hardly tell a lie about something so real in my own life, even though it was only a few hours old. So I muttered, in the quietest voice I could,

'Yes, I am.' I hoped no one else heard.

'Well, praise God, Dave Waite's a Christian!' Ding boomed loudly, and within seconds people were slapping me on the back and shaking my hand. Why are they getting so excited? I wondered. Anyway, I was a Christian now, and the world and his wife seemed to know about it. But what would my family say?

Mum was surprised when I shared with her what had happened during the week at Filey. Always having faith in God herself, she had been sad that only Terry seemed to share it. (Diana had adopted a 'wait and see' policy.) However, I still had to see Dad—and he was going to be the hardest to face.

I was nervous about it, and didn't know how to begin. In the end I decided just to apologise for the way I'd been acting. I told him I had really changed and that things would be different from now on. Dad looked at me in disbelief and then said,

'Look, son, I've been a policeman for twenty-odd years, and I know human nature through and through. I know that no one can change that much in seven days. I simply don't believe you. What's the catch?'

Now it was my turn to look amazed. I'd expected him to find it hard to forgive me, but it hadn't occurred to me that he might not believe me at all. I suppose that in spite of his many years of dealing with people, he hadn't come across Christian conversion before. Well, at least I had stated my intent, and he would just have to see. In fact, as time went on, the gap between me and Dad gradually narrowed, although it took a while for us to begin to trust each other.

I started going along with Philip and Trevor to 'Hope Hall', a Brethren Church on the outskirts of Warrington. I went to the Gospel Service in the evening, because the Sunday morning service was 'breaking of bread', or communion, and I wasn't able to participate because I hadn't been baptised, that is, totally immersed in water as an adult.

After the evening service we would all drive to a Christian coffee bar called 'The Fishnet', which was sponsored by various churches in the town. It was open to non-Christians, a place where you could drink coffee, listen to Christian rock groups playing gospel songs, and talk. I'd only been going for a week or two when I was asked by one of the leaders if I would stand up and 'give my testimony'. He wanted me to tell everyone what my life was like before I became a Christian, and how I'd changed.

That night there were a lot of bikers there, who were heckling everyone and making a lot of noise. The last thing I wanted to do was to stand up on a stage and talk to them.

'And now here's Dave,' said the leader, 'who's going to tell you how he came into a living relationship with the Lord Jesus Christ.'

The lads started to shout and catcall, making a terrible din. I was determined not to try and speak over their noise, so I put my mouth close to the microphone and shouted as loudly as I could, 'Shut up!'

My voice echoed through the speakers and everyone went quiet; the sheer volume and the ordinary non-religious language startled them. Unfortunately the silence unnerved me and my mind went blank. I stammered through a few words about how glad I was to be a Christian, and got off the stage as fast as possible.

Fortunately the guest speakers were more gifted than I was at public speaking, and many people heard the gospel in that coffee bar.

Each week the Christian organisers would gather for a prayer meeting before the coffee bar session. One evening I was passing the room when I heard someone praying—but not in English. I didn't recognise the language but it sounded very melodic and gentle. I waited outside for the stranger to finish, but at once someone else began—this time I recognised the voice, it was one of the local leaders—not in the same language but another one. I felt that I was intruding, so I crept away, but I was determined to find out what was going on.

I asked a few Christian friends, who explained that these people were 'speaking in tongues'—just like Jesus' disciples when they were given the 'gift of the Holy Spirit' as they waited together in the Upper Room. I hadn't come across this before, because Brethren doctrine suggested that this experience died with the disciples, and was no longer available to the church. Yet I had heard these men praying: were they 'speaking in tongues'?

I began to read books about baptism in the Holy Spirit, and as I read my Bible more carefully I began to find many references to the work and gifts of the Spirit.

By the time I had been a Christian for two years, I had been asked many times whether I wanted to be baptised—that is, totally immersed in water. My answer was always the same: I had been christened on the day I was born, although I hadn't known anything about it. Anyway, being baptised usually meant aligning oneself with a particular church or denomination, and I didn't want to do that. I felt that all Christian churches were valid, and I wanted to be part of the One Church, rather than a small section of it.

However, as I prayed about this, I began to notice an odd thing: although I followed a set scheme of study when I read my Bible each day, I seemed to come across more and more references to baptism. Every time I opened the Bible I was forced to think again about the issue. In the end I decided that I couldn't fight it any longer: God was showing me that he wanted me to be baptised.

Unlike the time when I became a Christian and tried to keep it a secret, this time I wanted everyone to know that I was going to be baptised. I decided it would be better to do it in Lymm, where I lived and worked, rather than in Warrington, where I had just a few friends. So I rang the minister of the Baptist Church in Lymm and asked if he would be willing to baptise me. I told him that I didn't want to become a member of that church, and explained my reasons. He was very understanding and invited me to call in and see him.

A few days later I visited him and found that a baptism had been arranged for that Easter, with one other candidate. The minister, George Cooper, was quite happy about my not joining the church if I chose not to, but explained that everyone needed a spiritual home, which didn't stop you having fellowship with other Christians as well.

I got a surprising reaction when I broke the news at home. Dad was very pleased and interested in what I was planning; I think my behaviour had convinced him that I was sincere in my beliefs, and that people really could change after all! It was Mum who found the news hard to take. She had been brought up in the Anglican tradition, and she couldn't understand why I suddenly wanted to be baptised. Hadn't all that been taken care of years ago, on the day I was born?

I tried to explain that this was a public witness and demonstration of something going on inside me, and that I had been guided to it by God, but she couldn't understand. She told me that she didn't want me to go through with it, and that if I did she wouldn't come to the service.

I sympathised with her feelings: until recently I would have said the same myself. Still, there was nothing for it. I was going to get baptised. All the same, I felt rather nervous: would I be able to go through with it? Would anyone turn up to the service? I had invited just about everyone I could think of.

When I arrived at the church I was heartened to see that the building was packed with people; I was also encouraged to see steam coming off the baptistry—I hate cold water!

I spoke a few words of testimony, then stepped into the water and felt myself being gently pushed backwards under the surface. As I emerged I experienced a tremendous surge of joy, and I knew that quite apart from this public witness to my conversion, a lot of my old life had been finally laid to rest.

Suddenly I was aware of someone running from the back of the church and throwing their arms around my wet shoulders.

'David, David, that was wonderful, I feel so proud of you.'

I blinked through the water still streaming down my face, but I didn't have to open my eyes to recognise that voice. It was my Mum, who had decided at the last moment to come along with Diana. She said afterwards it was the most moving service she had ever been to, and I was so glad she came that day.

In spite of my hesitation, I quickly got involved with the church in Lymm, realising that I could be a better witness in my own neighbourhood than in a church miles away. I made many new friends, including a man called Eric Stead, who helped me run the Boys' Brigade. He and his family lived close to us, so he often gave me a lift to meetings.

One Friday evening as I got in the car he asked hesitantly,

'David, have you ever heard of the baptism of the Holy Spirit?'

I said I had, and that I had several books on the subject, which I would lend to him if he was interested. In one of them there was a chapter on how to be baptised in the Holy Spirit: I'd read it carefully and done what it suggested, but nothing had happened. Eric warned me that he was a very slow reader, and I probably wouldn't see the book again for a few months, but I said I didn't mind—I'd finished with it.

I was greatly surprised, therefore, when he called round on the following Monday to return the book. His eyes were shining with happiness: he'd read it, he had been baptised in the Spirit, and now he was speaking in tongues! I would have found it hard to believe, but he was so full of joy I could see it was true.

I took the book back: maybe I hadn't finished with it after all.

I knew that my own faith wasn't as strong as it might be, so I decided to spend an hour in prayer each evening before going to bed. That way I could build up my relationship with the Lord, and maybe come up with some answers, too. Why hadn't anything happened when I prayed for the gift of tongues? Why was I still walking as badly as ever, even though I had prayed about my physical condition so many times? Perhaps I could find out.

Night after night I prayed and read the Bible. One night I was feeling particularly tired and depressed, and I began to wonder whether it was all worth it. Why didn't I just get into bed and go to sleep, like everyone else? I tried to pray, but felt as though my prayers bounced off the ceiling. It was all hopeless, and I was deluding myself. I would never be healed, never be baptised in the Spirit. What was the point of going on?

In my despair and frustration I started to cry—something I normally find it very difficult to do. But this evening tears came like a torrent, releasing all my pent-up feelings. I began to relax and to calm down, and to ask the Lord to forgive me for the things I'd been thinking. But I wasn't praying in English. The words that came out were foreign-sounding, and I stopped, alarmed. I started to pray again, this time in English, then half way through I changed to 'tongues'. I found I could pray in English or in tongues as I chose.

I was so happy I began to sing in tongues, and was fascinated at the sounds my mouth was producing. This wasn't the babbling of a baby, but a real language with structure and form, although I didn't understand a word of it. I knew that my spirit was filled with God's Spirit, and I felt closer to God than I had ever felt in my life.

6

New Beginnings

While all this was happening to me, Terry's life had undergone a change of direction, too. He became ill and spent some time in a military hospital; there he was visited regularly by members of the Church Army who made it part of their ministry to care for the men who were often far away from their families and friends. Terry was impressed by their witness and the scope of their ministry, and when it became clear that he would have to retire from the Guards for health reasons, he had already decided where he wanted to work next: he joined the Church Army.

He completed his training and moved to Bristol, where he became engaged to a lovely Irish girl called Frances. Their wedding took place in Belfast, and my mother, Diana and I travelled over to join them, but sadly Dad was too ill to travel.

Over the past few years Dad had become increasingly preoccupied with his claim against the Police Authority: he believed he had been wronged and wanted to put things right. Unfortunately his response to this stress was to smoke more and more heavily, and eventually lung cancer was diagnosed. His illness was long and painful, and a very difficult time for all the family.

Terry and Frances produced twin girls, and Dad loved to see them playing in the garden when Terry brought them up from Bristol to visit, but as time went on he grew too weak to join in with their games. The whole family helped to nurse him, and a few weeks before he died he made plain his own faith in Christ. I was so grateful that we had patched up our differences when we did, and that for the last few years of his life we were good friends.

Even though we were prepared for my father's death, it was still a shock, as such bereavements always are. In a sense, nothing can adequately prepare us for the finality of death. My mother's initial grief was followed by a sense of aimlessness and loss of purpose; all her adult life, it seemed, she had been a wife and mother—now her children were grown up and her husband gone. She found it hard to define her role in life. I understood her feelings, but felt that she needed to etch out a new life for herself, and gradually she began to do that. She became involved with women's organisations, voluntary work, and church activities, and I think that now she is busier than ever.

Meanwhile, Terry, to his delight, had discovered that his work took him overseas, and he and his family moved out to Uganda. They were destined to spend the next ten years there and in Rome, before they finally returned to the UK in 1979.

My own move was less spectacular, but quite as much of an upheaval for a homebody like me. It was provoked, indirectly, by my friend Eric.

He arrived one day with a book for me to read, assuring me that it was 'smashing'. I thanked him politely, though I doubted whether I would have time to sit down and read it—I was very busy at the office and at church these days.

I glanced at the title: *God's Smuggler* by Brother Andrew.

The book was about the plight of Christians in communist countries, and one man's mission to help them get Bibles, which were either illegal or very hard to obtain in most of the communist bloc. I was impressed by the courage and determination of Brother Andrew, and as there was an address at the end of the book, I decided to send a donation to the work. I was very surprised and pleased to receive a letter from Andrew's secretary a few days later, promising to add my name to the mailing list for his prayer letter.

Meanwhile I felt I wanted to do something. The book had fired me up: Christians in another part of the world were suffering, and surely there must be something I could do. I decided to copy Andrew; I would book a holiday to the Soviet Union, order some Russian Bibles and smuggle them into the country as Andrew had.

It was a good idea—but that's all it turned out to be. I booked a seven-day trip to Moscow, ordered the Bibles from a curious assistant at the local Bible Book Shop, and had all the necessary injections. I didn't tell anyone what I was doing, as I knew that my family and friends would only worry and try to stop me. It was in the days of currency restrictions, and I had trouble getting permission to take the necessary money out of the country. The injections made me feel ill, and to cap it all, the Russian Bibles I had ordered did not arrive in time. Even I could see the guidance the Lord was giving me, and I cancelled the trip.

However, I decided that even if I couldn't go to Russia, I could at least pray for Russian Christians. That summer Eric and I were helping to paint our church crypt, where the youth activities were held. When everyone else packed away their brushes and paint pots and went home, Eric and I would stay on and spend some time praying for Christians suffering persecution. I have no idea how God answered our prayers, but I believe strongly that those prayers were heard.

When I received Andrew's second prayer letter, I noticed that the British office of Open Doors was advertising for staff. I didn't think much about it, though it seemed to crop up in my prayers a lot over the next few weeks. When the third letter arrived I saw the job was still being advertised, so I applied for it. I was interviewed and went to Standlake in Oxfordshire to meet the team, and was subsequently offered the job.

I found it a hard decision to leave Lymm. A few years earlier I would have jumped at the chance to get away. Now things were different.

I enjoyed my work as Committee Clerk at the Council Offices: Lymm was growing, and it was interesting to attend all the Council meetings and know what decisions were being made for the future. The Clerk of the Council had a fatherly word with me about the security I was forsaking if I left the Council, with all its superannuation and pension schemes, and many of my colleagues urged me to think again.

It would be a difficult move socially, too. Since I became a Christian I had made a large circle of friends, and I knew I would miss them: I'm a very bad letter writer and I knew that in spite of all my efforts to keep in touch, things would never be the same.

Mum took the news very badly: with my father dead and Terry married, I was the man of the house, and she was going to miss me. Quite apart from that, she was concerned that the new job was very poorly paid compared with the one I was leaving. However, I had considered all these things and prayed about them. Every time I asked the Lord for his guidance, I felt the same reassurance that this was the right path to take: my Bible reading had constantly turned up scripture verses assuring me of God's love and protection.

I had nowhere to stay in Standlake, but I wrote to Noel Doubleday, the British Director of Open Doors, saying that I was prepared to sleep on the floor of the office if necessary! In the end Noel offered me a room in his house until I found somewhere to live.

Eric had a brother living in Abingdon, just a few miles from Standlake, and he offered to drive me there. Everything I possessed fitted on the back seat of his car, and we set off, waving goodbye to Mum. She was unable to hold back her tears as she realised what an uncertain future I was facing.

As we drove along we talked about my plans, and my decision to serve God in this way. Suddenly a large sheet of newspaper blew across the road and landed on the windscreen, clinging to the glass and completely obscuring Eric's view. After a moment it was torn off by the wind, and we breathed a sigh of relief.

'It's a good thing we're on the motorway,' said Eric. 'At least it's a straight road. As long as I kept going straight I knew we'd be all right, even though for a moment there I couldn't see the way ahead.'

'True,' I answered. 'That's just how I feel about this move: as long as I'm going along in God's will I'll be all right, even though I don't know what I'm getting into.'

We stayed the night with Eric's brother in Abingdon, and set off the next morning to Standlake. Noel and his wife Hilary made me feel very welcome when I arrived, to say nothing of their huge white Pyrenean mountain dog called Esther! I must admit that I felt a twinge of doubt as I watched Eric's car disappear out of sight, my last link with my life in Cheshire.

I soon settled into a new routine. Linda, the other staff member in my office, was a northerner like me, and soon made me feel at home. I did general organising work in the office, and handled the mountains of correspondence that came in. I had only been there a short while when many of the letters began to be about one topic: Christian involvement in the Olympic Games, to be held that year in Munich. Youth With a Mission—YWAM for short—planned to gather 1000 young people from thirty different countries as a Christian witness to the athletes and visitors in Germany. YWAM is an American organisation, headed by a man for whom I have tremendous respect and regard, Loren Cunningham.

'Brother Andrew is a guest speaker,' said Linda one morning as we took our coffee break. 'Have you thought of going? I'm sure Noel would let you have the time off.'

I was surprised; I hadn't thought of going to the Olympics. It would be great fun, but I didn't know anyone else who would be there.

The next Sunday at church I was talking to Andy Hall, a tall young man in the RAF at Brize Norton. He told me that his sister Alison was planning to join the YWAM event in Munich. A week or two later I met Alison herself, and realised that I had already been writing to her as she supported the work at Open Doors.

We chatted for a while and promised to keep in touch, just in case I decided to go to Munich; however, as usual, I didn't get round to it.

By the end of July I began to think seriously about going to the Olympics in August, but I realised that I had left things far too late to organise the trip. Still, I felt that if the Lord wanted me to go, he would make it possible, so I prayed that he would show me his will. I was surprised at the way my prayers were answered.

The Open Doors office was well known to many British Christians, and people often called in for books or tracts when they were going to Eastern European countries. One visitor was Geoffrey Gould, who called in one day. He was a well-built man in his early fifties, with untidy hair and a handlebar moustache, wearing an open-necked shirt and corduroy trousers.

'Geoffrey, how good to see you,' said Linda, getting up. 'This is David, our new recruit.'

'Well, praise the Lord, praise the Lord,' said Geoffrey, slapping me on the back. 'I've just come to pick up some books and things as I'm off to Munich for the Games next week. I was hoping to take someone with me in the car, but everyone who wants to go seems to have got fixed up.' Wondering why we had all gone silent, he looked up from the pile of tracts he was collecting, to find us all staring at him.

Quickly I explained that I wanted to go to Munich but had no way of getting there, and he just happened to be the answer to my prayers!

We set off for Munich in Geoff's Volvo Estate car, though our progress wasn't as rapid as I expected: he wanted to call in and see a friend here, make a slight detour to meet a friend there. Geoff seemed to know half the Christians in the south of England! He assured me, however, that he knew a good place to stay that evening, if we missed the ferry we were heading for. Predictably, we did miss it: the 'good place' turned out to be a spinney just off the main coast road.

'No sense in paying good money for hotels when we've got the car to sleep in, eh?' said Geoffrey.

We caught the ferry the next day, and after a wonderful drive across the continent we finally arrived at Hurlach Castle, the headquarters of YWAM for the Munich Games.

The castle was originally built to house a wealthy family and their servants, and it was now massively overcrowded. There were 700 of us based there, with 300 Americans further up the village.

Because I arrived late there was no room left for me, though Geoffrey had secured his place weeks before. There was only one solution: for the next three weeks I would have to sleep in the car! Actually, when I saw the cramped conditions inside the castle—three-tier bunk beds, fifty to a room—I decided I probably had the better deal.

I was feeling scruffy and dirty after my journey, but as I headed indoors to wash, I bumped into Alison Hall, my one contact from England. She had arrived in a far more civilised manner by air a little while earlier, and already seemed to know what was going on. Apparently we were to be grouped into teams of twenty, and the idea was that one day half the groups would go out into Munich, giving out tracts and talking to people about Jesus, while the others stayed at the castle having teaching sessions and praying for those in the town.

Apart from my lack of accommodation, one of the biggest challenges was the food. Catering in those conditions for so many different nationalities was a nightmare, and the basic fare seemed to be peanut butter and jelly sandwiches (peanut butter and jam to the British). This was familiar food for the Americans, but it seemed to me to be the most disgusting combination I could think of. Most of the British team lost weight in those three weeks as we gave away our sandwiches to our hungry American cousins.

Alison and I discovered that against all the odds we had been put in the same team. As we travelled by train from Hurlach to Munich, we got into conversation with two of our team-mates, Lee Vickers and Jenny James. We discovered that as we had prayed about the trip, each of us felt that God wanted us to go into the Olympic Village to contact the athletes. I had brought some Russian Bibles with me, and I wanted to give them to the Russian athletes.

Once in Munich we made our way to the Olympic Village, wondering what to do. We knew that guards were posted to stop unauthorised people from entering the village, but we were sure the Lord would open a way for us. One thing was for sure—we wouldn't be mistaken for athletes! I walked with a very bad limp, and my upper body was twisted; all the others didn't exactly look fit, either.

We prayed for a while, and then someone suggested that we open our Bibles and see if the Lord would guide us in that way. Ali opened her Bible at Isaiah 35:3, 'Strengthen the weak hands, steady the knees that give way.' Wasn't the Russian church weak, and in need of help, as it was driven to its knees? We read on, comforted by other verses: 'Say to those with fearful hearts, "Be strong, do not fear" ' (v 3); 'Then will the eyes of the blind be opened and the ears of the deaf unstopped' (v 5); 'Then will the lame leap like a deer' (v 6).

We felt that this was God's guidance through his word. After all, if he could open blind eyes, surely he could close seeing ones for a few minutes! We decided to walk towards the guards at the entrance. As we approached, the guards turned away, seeming not to notice us. Amazingly, we all walked past them.

Once inside, we began to laugh with relief and thank the Lord, but as we turned the next corner we were confronted by yet another gateway and more guards! From the main entrance this second set were not visible.

I told everyone just to walk calmly ahead, as we had at the first gate, but Ali began to lose her nerve. She began to wonder whether we were right in what we were doing, and her faith in the project wavered. The guards must have sensed this, because they let three of us through, but challenged Ali. I turned around and saw the look of dismay on her face.

'Stop—they've got Ali,' I said, and the three of us stood some distance away and started to pray in tongues. A moment later Ali was walking through to join us. She had told the guards she had business in the Village and showed them her Bible and her YWAM pass.

'I could see you all praying,' she said, 'and they told me to go back. Instead I just walked towards you, and they ignored me.'

We were all inside the Village—but that was just the start.

7

The Olympic Village

Once we were actually inside the Village it was as though
we had entered a different world. All the buildings had been
specially built for the Games and were sparkling white. The
weather was very warm and sunny and we strolled along,
feeling quite out of place, but full of anticipation. The
people we passed came from all over the world, but they
had one thing in common—they were all superbly fit!

Every so often along the road there would be little stalls
offering health drinks and yoghurts. Everything was free as
the firms there were interested in promoting their products.
We offered to pay, feeling we should tell these people that
we weren't connected with the Games, but they insisted
that we try them, free of charge. Everything was delicious
and refreshing, and best of all, there wasn't a peanut butter
and jelly sandwich in sight!

We couldn't just walk around all day, fascinating though
it was: we had a job to do, but we weren't sure how to go
about it. Someone suggested we open a Bible again to look
for guidance. This wasn't something any of us usually
did—spotting verses at random—but somehow our whole

situation was so unusual that we felt that unusual methods were called for.

This time we turned up Acts 21 and 22, where Paul preached at length to the crowds outside the Temple. Was the Lord asking us to find a church and preach outside it? It seemed highly unlikely that there should be a church in the Olympic Village, but we could at least look.

After wandering around for a while we sat down on a bench to rest, with our backs leaning against a warm brick wall. Two athletes jogged by in brilliant electric blue track-suits, and I waved to them.

'Excuse me,' I began hesitantly, 'do you know if there's a church in the Village, and how we get there?'

They looked at me incredulously.

'Sure, there's a church here. You're sitting right outside it!'

We looked more closely at the wall we were leaning against, and sure enough there was a small sign indicating that this was a church. Clearly we were still going along with the Lord's plan for that day. We went inside, and found the building very cool and quiet. We thanked the Lord for leading us safely here, and Lee took two Russian Bibles and placed them near the altar, trusting that the right people would find them. What now?

We remembered the verse about Paul preaching to the crowds—so although there were no crowds nearby we decided we had better go outside and hope that we could attract someone to speak to.

We should have realised that the Lord was working on our behalf. The first thing we saw when we stepped outside was a camera crew, setting up just opposite the church. Jenny suggested that we sing a few Christian songs, and at once the crew stopped chatting, put out their cigarettes, and started filming us! Facing the church was a large block of flats with balconies, and several people came out to see what the music was and why we were being filmed. Other people passing stopped too, and suddenly we had our crowd!

We each took a turn at speaking to the group that had assembled, and then after a few minutes we would break into song again. The first group of people drifted off, to be replaced by others. An American Christian stopped to speak to us, and suggested that some people might be turned off rather than helped by our actions. We agreed that what we were doing was rather unorthodox, but explained that we had been shown specifically by the Lord what to do that day.

When we had finished our impromptu service, we realised that we still had some more Russian Bibles with us, so we set off for the Russian athletes' accommodation. This building looked just like all the others, with one exception. Two beefy-looking men stood outside, scrutinising everyone who entered or left. They had clearly been placed there to keep a strict eye on any contacts the Russian athletes might make.

We couldn't believe that the Lord would bring us this far and not allow us to deliver the Bibles—but how could we get past the men at the door? The only weapon we had was prayer, so we huddled together and asked the Lord to help us in our task. Jesus said in Mark 3:27 that anyone who wishes to enter a strong man's house must first tie up the strong man. We felt that what we had to do was to bind the atheistic forces behind these Russian guards and render them helpless.

We prayed, and then looked on, half in disbelief, as the men dropped their watchful attitude and walked away! Several Russian athletes came out, so we chatted to them for a while. Eventually they left, and the place seemed deserted. We were free to go in.

In the entrance lobby was a table with letters and papers for the athletes to collect. We put the Bibles there in such a way that they were not apparent if someone just glanced at the table, but they would be noticed when the mail was collected.

It was now getting late, so we decided we should leave the Village. We had something to eat at yet another wayside stall, and were making our way back towards the gates when we became aware of a commotion a little way ahead. We pushed through a crowd of excited people, to find a huge bear of a man doing a kind of Indian war dance! I asked someone what was going on, and they told me he was Russian, and had just won the gold medal for weight lifting. I was standing right next to him by this time, so I slapped him on the back and said, 'Congratulations!' I don't know whether he understood what I said, but he suddenly produced the medal which was the cause of all the excitement and gave it to me to hold.

In that very special moment I realised afresh that there is no fundamental difference between nationalities. We all have our own moments of delight and excitement, sorrow and despair. We are all loved by the same God, who wants us to love him in return. I wished I had a Bible left to give that man, but was glad to think of the books lying safely waiting at the Russian quarters.

At last we made our way out of the Village, praying again that we would not be stopped and questioned by the guards, and took the train back to Hurlach Castle, with quite a tale to tell.

When we told our team-mates what we had been able to do, it encouraged others to do the same. Some did get in, though others were stopped and turned back. Still, Bibles and books were reaching many of the athletes.

After a while, the days seemed to fall into a kind of routine, though the things we were doing were in themselves far from routine. It was exciting to go out onto the streets, talking to people about the way God could help them in their lives, and just as exciting in a different kind of way to stay at the castle and listen to people like Brother Andrew, Loren Cunningham and Corrie Ten Boom (author of The Hiding Place), who spoke at one of the final evening sessions. She held up an embroidered cloth, showing us the back of it. All we could see were the crossed-over threads and knots—it was quite ugly.

'Isn't this beautiful?' she asked us, and then added, 'oh, but of course, you can't see the side I can see, can you? Let me turn it round.'

She reversed the cloth to show a beautiful crown embroidered in gold, silver and purple. She then explained that when circumstances in life seem ugly and without purpose, it is important to remember the other side—the side God sees. Maybe we will never know, on earth, why we go through some experiences, but one day God will show us the finished piece of our life, made beautiful by him.

Life at the castle did have its lighter moments, though. Each night as other people settled down in their over-crowded rooms, I scrambled into my sleeping bag and stretched out on the front seat of Geoffrey's car. One morning I was woken very early, while it was still dark, because Geoffrey needed to go and pick up someone who was stranded somewhere. I was half asleep, and none of it seemed to make much sense, but I obligingly rolled out of Geoff's car and into another one nearby, while Geoff roared off into the darkness. I fell asleep again instantly.

The next thing I knew it was broad daylight, and people were passing all around the car on their way to breakfast. I suddenly realised that all my clothes were still in Geoff's car. As the nights were hot, I wasn't wearing anything inside the sleeping bag: I couldn't walk anywhere in it, and I couldn't walk anywhere without it!

People kept giving me a friendly wave as they passed the car, but no one stopped to chat. At last I spotted Ruth and Heinz, a married couple, and calling them over I explained my problem. It took me a while to convince them that I wasn't joking, but they agreed to lend me some clothes.

Eventually I was released from my imprisonment, and with wrists and ankles protruding from Heinz's jumper and trousers (Heinz was much smaller than I was) I hurried off to breakfast.

We found a good deal of fun and fellowship among the young people of all nationalities gathered at the castle. There was anticipation in the air throughout those three weeks: we believed that God could answer prayer—and that he would. At the end of the second week the reservoir that supplied the village of Hurlach had almost been drained, because of the extra visitors. The weather had been hot and sunny for weeks, and the village council warned Loren Cunningham that the area was heading for a drought.

With his wife and a few others Loren began to pray, on a day of brilliant sunshine and blue skies. As the afternoon wore on the sky darkened and with very little warning a heavy rainstorm broke over our heads. By the time the rain stopped, the reservoir was replenished and the problem solved. People were laughing and joking as they came back to the castle, enjoying the warm summer rain.

Then, towards the end of our stay, came the tragic events for which the Munich Olympics will always be remembered. Israeli athletes were taken hostage and murdered.

The whole mood of the Games changed: the atmosphere of happy optimism was gone. Until then, people had been saying how good it was finally to have settled with the horrors of the Second World War. A new generation was able to meet, nation with nation, without those memories at the forefront of their minds. After the shooting, German people were weeping openly in the streets at the horror of what had happened at the Games. Murder had been done— not just to athletes, but to Jewish athletes.

The Christians went about trying to bring comfort to those who were so distressed, and some good did come out of the tragedy. Up until then the mayor of Munich had refused permission for a Christian march of witness through the town. Now he contacted Loren Cunningham and agreed. He said that we were the only ones with any hope left for the world.

So for a whole afternoon we sang and walked through the town, and then a united service was held in one of the town squares, involving all the various Christian organisations—some 2500 people. That evening we were invited to use the hill next to the Olympic Stadium for an open air service. Holding lighted candles, we formed the shape of the cross together: a cross of flames that could be seen for several miles. We walked around the Olympic complex singing 'Jesus loves you, Jesus loves you.' There were thousands of dots of light shining in the darkness, witnessing to the Light of the world. It was an unforgettable sight.

All too soon it was time to start thinking about returning to England: Geoff was planning to spend a short holiday in Europe, so I had to get home alone. One morning I saw a card pinned on a noticeboard, offering for sale a plane ticket to London. One of Alison's friends had also decided to stay on in Germany. It seemed a good idea to buy it—especially as her seat was next to Ali's!

Although Ali and I seemed to get on really well together, this put me in something of a dilemma. I had decided years before that marriage was not for me. I had seen so many people marry, who were plainly unsuited to each other, and within months they would be wishing they hadn't, or worse still getting divorced. I was sure I could be a much better witness for Christ unmarried, and whenever a relationship started to get serious I would make my views known; usually that ended any budding friendship. I thought about Ali a lot, but I was determined that my friendship with her would end when we left Munich—unless the Lord showed me specifically that it should continue.

I was encouraged by the fact that out of the 1,000 young people in Hurlach, we had been put in the same team; also, whenever we had worked together (for instance in the Olympic Village) the Lord seemed to support and bless us. Was the air ticket a sign from God? If anything as serious as marriage was to be contemplated, we had to be very sure.

We flew back to England together and exchanged addresses, both secretly hoping we would meet again one day. We even walked hand in hand across the tarmac after we disembarked, little knowing that we were being observed by all the people waiting at the airport. Ali's Mum and Dad must have wondered who on earth was the scruffy individual with a three-weeks' beard and a bad limp who was holding their daughter's hand!

When I got home I found a message waiting for me: Terry's wife Frances was in London with the children, and wanted to know if I would like to see them all before they went back to Rome. Unfortunately her relatives didn't have room to put me up too—did I know anyone I could stay with in London? The answer was obvious: Alison. The Lord seemed to be turning all my plans to stay a bachelor upside down.

As far as marriage went, I wasn't much of a catch: I had always set little store by material possessions, and had given away any money I didn't immediately need. My salary at Open Doors hardly supported me, let alone a wife. In addition I was disabled, had nowhere to live, and had no long-term prospects or plans!

Alison didn't seem to notice any of this, and if she did notice she didn't seem to mind. She worked at a boarding school for emotionally disturbed children in Surrey: she loved the work and cared deeply for the children, and some of them had found a faith in Jesus for themselves. It was wearing work, though, and when she visited me at weekends, often the first thing she did was to dissolve into tears.

We started to pray for each other, for her in her demanding job, and for me amid the pressures and tensions of the missionary society. It became a joke among our friends that however little time we were able to spend together, Ali and I would always find time to pray. Ieuan and Irene, the couple with whom I was now lodging, were very kind to us, and let Alison stay whenever she wanted. Sometimes I visited her at her parents' home in Purley, and shared in their family life with Andy when he was home on leave, and her younger sister Penny.

Marriage, however, was a different matter. I was still very unwilling to consider it, though everything seemed to point that way: our aims in life were identical, and we thought alike on so many issues. Would my feelings for Ali just 'wear off' after a while and leave us both stranded? Was I just feeling homesick for the friends I left behind in Lymm? Was I just running from the old loneliness which had haunted me all my life? I simply didn't know.

When Ali announced that she was attending a course and couldn't come and visit me for a couple of weeks, I decided to use the time to find out once and for all what the Lord intended for us. Were we to marry or not? I intended to fast and pray until I got the answer!

My behaviour caused some confusion in the Davies household, because although Ieuan and Irene understood what I was doing, they had no idea of the problem I was wrestling with. For a whole fortnight I agonised over the matter, taking days to fast and pray at intervals. In the end I was sure that it was right for me to ask Alison to marry— the only trouble was, I had no assurance of what the answer would be.

I decided that on her next visit I would wait for the right moment over the weekend: in the event I proposed a few minutes after she arrived! She hesitated for about five seconds before saying 'Yes', which was just about all the suspense I could stand. The month was November, and I wanted to be married by Christmas; luckily Ali had more sense, and we decided on an August wedding.

8

Touched by God

Although we were now engaged to be married, Ali and I could still see each other only at weekends, if we were lucky. For some time life went on very much as it had before Munich, except for the long telephone calls we had each evening.

However, one evening after our engagement I went with Ieuan to a meeting at the Swindon House Church which I attended. When we arrived the room was packed, but we managed to find a seat in a corner. The meeting was very lively, with lots of Christian choruses being sung over and over again by the people crowded into the room, who obviously had a real love for Jesus. By this time, I had been a Christian for eight years, and this was a familiar scene.

This meeting was unusual, though, because a guest speaker had been invited. Ian Andrews was a tall thin man with fair curly hair; he spoke softly and hesitantly, quite unlike any evangelical speaker I had ever heard. He began the meeting with a talk on the power of God, pointing out that Jesus, risen from the dead, could do the same things today, through his church, that he did when he was on earth.

He referred to 1 Corinthians 12:8: 'For to one is given by the Spirit the word of wisdom; to another the word of knowledge by the same Spirit. To another faith by the same Spirit; to another the gifts of healing by the same Spirit' (AV). The Lord then began to give Ian 'words of knowledge' about the needs of people who were present.

Ian said that the Lord was telling him that there was someone in the room who had a back problem: a man stood up and acknowledged that was so. Ian prayed with him, and his pain disappeared. Next, he spoke of a hearing problem; sure enough, a lady came forward, and after a few moments of prayer she was able to discard her hearing aid. I was delighted and sceptical all at once: I was glad to see the relief these people were receiving, but a part of me could hardly believe my eyes. Surely it couldn't be that easy. On and on it went. Many people were being healed that night, whether or not I doubted it.

Ian seemed to wait for a word of knowledge before offering to pray for anyone, but towards the end of the meeting he asked if anyone wanted to come out for prayer. Ieuan urged me in a kind of stage whisper to go forward, but I sat firmly where I was. Life had taught me not to draw attention to myself, and anyway I knew that the disappointment would be huge if I was prayed for and nothing happened.

When the meeting was over, however, someone must have pointed me out to Ian, for he came over and asked if I would like him to pray for me. I mumbled something about my disabled leg, and he repeated his question. Profoundly sceptical, I agreed, and we went into another room together.

I sat on a dining chair, and Ian said he was going to ask Jesus to touch me in some way. He told me to relax and close my eyes and start to thank Jesus for what he was going to do. I closed my eyes and almost at once I felt a hand start to massage my heel—but it somehow felt as though it was being rubbed from the inside. Curious, I opened my eyes, and found that no one was touching me. I told Ian what I had felt, and he asked if I could do anything now that I couldn't do before. I found to my surprise that I could wiggle my toes! This information was greeted with cheers from the others who had followed us into the room.

Ian then looked at the considerable difference in the length of my legs, and announced that he was going to pray for them to be the same. He asked some of the men to come and support my legs so that they were stretched out side by side, and told me to close my eyes and thank Jesus for what he was going to do. Then he prayed quietly, but with real authority: 'In the name of Jesus I command this leg to grow.'

Everyone started to pray with Ian, when suddenly Ieuan shouted,

'There it goes now!' as he felt my leg move down inside the trouser leg! It was a strange moment: I knew something supernatural was happening, but it felt so normal that I kept thinking, Why hasn't this happened before?

I stood up, and the improvement was dramatic. My leg felt longer and stronger than it had ever done, and of course my walking was greatly improved. We gave thanks and praised God, until Ian said,

'I don't believe the Lord has finished with you yet. How about that arm of yours?'

My right arm had been affected in a similar way to my leg, and was thinner and shorter than the other.

Again Ian prayed, but this time I didn't close my eyes.

'In the name of Jesus,' he said, 'I command this arm to grow.' And with my own eyes I watched my right arm grow to the same length and strength as the left. If I had ever had any doubts about the power or the love of God, they were gone for good. God was there, and he had proved it in a very loving way. My leg had grown to such an extent that eighteen months later I was able to have an operation on my Achilles tendon, which meant that I could put my heel on the ground for the first time in my life! It also meant that I could wear normal shoes instead of boots—which up till then had been the only footwear which would stay on my misshapen foot.

Once I had experienced the love of God in this way, it was difficult for me to doubt his existence, or his ability to heal. Of course I am aware of those who pray for healing but find that nothing happens (remember I was in that category myself for a long time). If you were to meet me now you would see that there are still things that the Lord needs to touch in my body to make me physically fit—I still walk with a slight limp—but whether he chooses to heal me completely is up to him.

This experience gave me great faith to pray for others, but the first time I did so it had an unusual result. I was working in the British office of Open Doors, and a student called Carol was giving us some temporary help. Carol was a pleasant, helpful girl with short brown hair and glasses.

One day she said that she had a really bad headache, and I suggested that we should pray about it, rather than that she should take a painkiller. I prayed a very simple prayer, asking the Lord to take her headache away, and she went out of the office shortly afterwards. A few minutes later she came rushing back, bursting with excitement.

'Dave, guess what,' she cried. 'After you prayed for me, I put my glasses back on, and everything was fuzzy, as though they weren't mine. I took them off and I could see clearly—when I put them back on my vision was blurred.'

I looked at her open-mouthed.

'Dave, don't you understand?' she demanded. 'I don't need my glasses any more. In fact, I can't wear them any more!'

After that my confidence about praying for others and seeing them healed began to grow. I was beginning to find more and more that God delights in being taken at his word in the Bible. As Jesus said, 'You may ask me for anything in my name, and I will do it' (Jn 14:14).

In fact, several years were to pass before the gift of healing became important to us again.

We were attending a house fellowship in Witney, and one evening I saw with delight that Ian Andrews had been invited as a guest speaker. I wanted Ali to meet him, as she had been as thankful as I was for the healing which had taken place in me.

Ian gave a short Bible study, and followed it with several words of knowledge. I was impressed once again by a sense of the presence of God, and the privilege of watching him at work. As the meeting was about to close, Ian invited people to come forward if they wished to receive a blessing. I went forward with several others, and as Ian placed his hand on my head I felt myself falling backwards! I must have been caught by those behind me, for I was laid gently on the carpet, stretched out like a corpse. However, my body was far from corpse-like: the moment I touched the carpet, I started to tremble violently. I was aware of this, but felt as though I was in a dream: I could hear what was going on, and could have opened my eyes and got up at any moment I chose, but I knew God was doing something in me, and I didn't want to move.

The others at the meeting gathered round me and started to praise God, praying and singing. The trembling went on for about ten minutes, then suddenly stopped. I got up and went back to my seat, feeling very relaxed and at peace. It wasn't until later that night, as I was undressing for bed, that I realised what had been going on.

Because of the difficulty I had always had with walking, leaning sideways to accommodate the shorter leg, I had become very pigeon chested, and my upper body was twisted. Now, however, as I took off my shirt, the change became apparent. My body was straight, my chest was normal, and the top of my right leg was now firm and strong like the other! I had gone out that night to meet God, but I had received a much greater blessing than I had expected.

These events strengthened my faith, and after a while I wanted to share what I had learned about God with others. I began to lead Bible studies and worship meetings myself, and found that the Lord would sometimes give me words of knowledge for people who were present.

On one occasion Ali and I were asked to lead a house-party in North Wales for a week. Each evening I would give a Bible study, and afterwards I spoke to individuals as the Lord gave me words of knowledge about their circumstances. Some people wanted to deepen their relationship with God; others needed to receive forgiveness in some area of their lives; others still were looking for healing. We watched amazed as the Lord gave one lady sight in her blind eye, released another from arthritis, and caused a leg to lengthen just like mine.

When the Holy Spirit gives me a word of knowledge, he usually puts in my body a symptom of what the person is experiencing. So if someone has back pain, I will suddenly feel that pain, and know that the Lord wants to touch someone with that problem. Because of this, I can usually point to the exact spot which is affected—because it is affecting me! As the person acknowledges that particular 'word', and they receive their healing from the Lord, the symptoms in me go away too. I admit it sounds unusual, but it has happened too many times for me to doubt that it comes from God.

Sometimes the words of knowledge from the Lord are very specific, but no one claims them: then I ask God for more information, and hope someone will have the confidence to respond.

One Sunday I was preaching in a small Methodist church near where I live, but where I knew almost no one in the congregation. Half way through my message I realised that the Lord was telling me there was someone present who suffered with pain in their hands. I hesitated, not wanting to interrupt myself, but felt that I was being urged by God to speak.

Feeling somewhat self-conscious I said, 'I believe the Lord is showing me there is someone here who has pain in their hands.' Some people looked a little surprised, but no one responded. I asked God silently for something to add to this. 'I believe it could be arthritis.' Still no one spoke. I turned again to the Lord for more details. He showed me that the person was taking two red tablets twice a day, and when there was still silence, that they kept a little cut-glass beaker of water by the bed with the tablets!

I was sure that someone present must recognise all this description, but when nothing happened I gave it up and continued with my message. After the meeting an elderly lady approached me, and said, 'I think what you were saying may have been for me.' Her hands were twisted with arthritis, and she said she was taking red tablets in a glass just like the one I described. I asked why she had said nothing in the meeting: she answered, 'I wasn't sure it was me you were talking about.'!

We did pray for her later, and she did indeed experience some improvement in her condition, but I couldn't help feeling that an opportunity had been missed. I remembered my own reluctance at the first meeting I went to: our British reserve, and our doubts about God's ability to work in this way, can rob us of so much.

I feel I must add a qualification here. I know from personal experience that the Lord works in the way I have described; however, great damage can be done by people who take too simplistic a view of all this, and who believe that all they have to do is to pray for instant healing. I myself have too often been the victim of over-zealous people who insist on praying for me without a leading from the Holy Spirit: when nothing has happened they have been embarrassed, and I have been hurt and angry.

I am always very careful about the words of knowledge I speak: every one has always been acknowledged by the person concerned or by someone close to them. My rule is that if you are unsure about praying for someone, you should not do so; if you promise infallible healing and are proved wrong, you should be prepared to pick up the pieces of disappointment and damaged faith afterwards.

9

Moving Experiences

At last the long-awaited day of our wedding arrived. The service was held at Purley Baptist Church, near Alison's family home, and her parents had arranged a reception for 120 guests. However, when I arrived at the church, it was packed: over 350 people had come just to join us for the service, many of them all the way from Lymm. It was good to see so many familiar faces in the congregation, and to hear the great wave of sound from behind us as we sang the hymns. I found the service very moving and it made a deep impression on me. For us there were no thoughts of 'I hope it works out for us'; what we were doing that day was to be for ever. It was a solemn moment.

Ali and I had both been Christians for several years before we were married, and we were used to relying on God in our daily lives. It made marriage seem a great adventure, as we set out on our new life together, eager to see what God had in store for us; we trusted him to care for us and guide us together just as he had in our single lives.

Ali had of course given up her job in Surrey, and came to be part of the team at Open Doors with me; we knew that in time the missionary society was planning to send us both out to work in Austria. It was because of this that Ali's parents had arranged our honeymoon in Austria, so that we could have a look at the place where we would eventually be living.

It was a marvellous holiday; the scenery was wonderful, and so was the company! It was great to be together all the time, instead of for a few snatched hours. We talked and talked, catching up on all the things there had never been time to say.

One day we decided to go to the top of one of the mountains; as we were both incredibly unfit, we took the cable car to the top. The view was superb, and the whole area very peaceful: there was no one around except for a few cows with enormous bells around their necks, and a few people in the tiny cafe which closed when the last cable car left at night.

We strolled about, still talking hard, and though Ali said after a while that she thought we ought to be getting back, of course I knew better! When eventually we did wander back, it was to find that the last cable car had already left.

Ali was worried, thinking that we would have to spend the night up there on the mountain, but I told her to calm down—there was bound to be another way down the mountain. I consulted the cafe owner, who seemed surprised to see us.

'Yes, sir,' he said with a grin, 'there is another way down.' He paused while I gave Ali a kind of I-told-you-so smile.

'What is it?' I asked.

'You walk!' he replied.

We stared at each other in dismay. Neither of us had much physical stamina, and we certainly weren't dressed for mountain walking. However, as there was only about an hour before nightfall, we decided to set off straight away. Almost immediately Ali tripped, and since we were holding hands, we both went crashing down.

At this point we decided that we ought to pray about this enforced walk of ours, and we took to our hearts the verse in the Bible which says that God sends his angels so that our feet will not stumble (Ps 91:11). We walked on confidently after that, and although some of the cliffs were terrifying, we reached the bottom in safety.

When we got back from the honeymoon we had a problem—where were we going to live? We were not due to go out to Austria for some time yet, and buying a house on my small salary from Open Doors was out of the question. Because I had never anticipated marriage, and believed in supporting Christian ventures and individuals as much as possible, my savings were deliberately almost always nil.

Our first home was a lovely 300-year-old cottage in Standlake. The owners were going to America for three months, and asked if we would like to rent it. They were rather nervous about this, as previous tenants had failed to leave on the agreed date, but we assured them that we would keep any promise about leaving.

It was lovely living in the old cottage; it had a fireplace so huge that you could stand in it and look up at the sky. We spent our first Christmas there, inviting both families to join us—there were so many people sitting round the table that Ali and I ate our first Christmas dinner together off a little serving trolley.

At the end of the three months we knew we would have to move, and we were concerned as Standlake is such a small place that there wasn't likely to be much accommodation available. However, just two weeks before our time ran out I had a visit from Pam, the local postmistress. The flat over the post office was vacant—but only for a while, as it would be needed as soon as a new shop manager was appointed. Would we be interested? We hesitated before agreeing; we had paid the rent at the cottage from Ali's last teaching pay cheque, and we doubted whether we would be able to afford the £60 or so this flat would cost.

Pam must have read our minds.

'Because we will only be able to give you a few days' notice, Jimmy and I thought we ought to reduce the rent. We thought about £5 a month.'

'£5 a month! That's ridiculous!' we chorused. Even with the limitations she had put on the tenancy, she could have asked for far more, and we didn't want to take advantage of her generosity. In the end we compromised, and the flat was ours until further notice for the princely sum of £5 a week!

Our new home had a large and sunny living room, a kitchen, bathroom and small bedroom, and a large bedroom which was situated right over the post office counter. If we lazed in bed on a Saturday when the post office was open, the banging of the stamp on postal orders and pensions sounded as if someone was running up the stairs to the flat. It was useful, too, living over the only shop in the village—especially on one disastrous evening when a friend was coming to dinner. The stew Alison had prepared slipped out of her hands onto the kitchen floor, and we had to rush downstairs and buy a replacement meal!

The only drawback to the flat was that supplies and cardboard boxes were stored in a room below our living room; when Alison became pregnant the smell made her nauseous.

When Mum heard that Alison was pregnant she asked if she could come and visit us in Standlake, as she had something important to say to me.

'Now that you're to be a father soon, David, there's something I have to tell you about your own birth,' she said. She explained about the death of my twin, and how she and Dad had kept it a secret so as not to upset the other children. I felt a strange sensation of relief.

'You've not really told me anything new,' I replied. 'It just confirms what I've felt all my life.'

Now at last I began to understand myself and the strange emotions I had battled with since infancy: the deep loneliness, the search for friendships, and the discovery that even the closest friendship didn't satisfy the feeling that a part of me was missing. Becoming a Christian had helped; knowing Jesus and the Holy Spirit had filled some of the void in me, and my marriage had given me a wonderful companion and friend as well as a loving wife. But just occasionally I still got those unexplained feelings of missing someone; now at last I knew what they meant, and could deal with them rationally.

Thirteen months after our marriage, our first son, Daniel, was born. Those 'few days' notice on the flat never caught up with us, and we were able to stay there until six weeks after Daniel's birth, when we left to live and work in Austria.

Part of the work of Open Doors was to help people who wished to take Bibles and other Christian literature into areas where such material is illegal or at least very hard to obtain. The British office had decided to establish a kind of 'safe house' where people en route to the Eastern bloc could stay for a while; we would keep a stock of Bibles and tracts in various languages. At the same time we worked among the local people—mostly Yugoslavian immigrants in very poor housing, who were working in Austria temporarily so as to raise money for their families at home. We enjoyed our work, and loved meeting people, both the Austrians and Yugoslavs who lived around us, and the British and others who passed through our home.

Living in Austria was a challenge to us both in many ways, but one of our biggest problems was lack of finance. It wasn't that the British office of Open Doors didn't pay us—it was just that the money was always being held up in Vienna or somewhere, and failing to reach us on time. We would go along to our bank and try to draw out some cash, only to be told at the counter that our account was empty! Then we would make urgent phone calls to England, and sometimes the money would arrive quickly—and sometimes slowly. It wasn't until we were about to leave Austria that we discovered that most of the time the money had been paid into the wrong account.

The one Christmas we spent in Austria was almost a disaster because of this problem. The English office rang us to say that two Americans would be passing through, and please would we put them up for Christmas. We were pleased to have some English-speaking company for the holiday, and went to the bank to draw out some cash. Yet again, no funds were available. If we had just been catering for ourselves, Ali, Daniel and I would have done without any kind of celebration, but we wanted to make our American guests welcome with gifts and decorations. We felt bad at offering such a mean Christmas to these people we hadn't even met.

Ali sat on our bed, counting the few grochen in her purse, and trying to look brave. We prayed about it, but we couldn't see how the Lord could answer our prayers; transactions were slowing up because of the holiday and the office hadn't held out much hope of getting money to us.

That evening we had a visit from two Finnish missionary friends of ours, Pekka and Matti, who were doing the same kind of work as us. They were on their way home to Finland and had dropped in to wish us a Merry Christmas.

We gave them coffee and were asking about their plans, when suddenly Pekka interrupted and asked, 'Is everything all right?'

'Yes,' I said, 'fine.' I trusted the Lord to deal with our problem, and didn't want to worry our friends with it.

Pekka looked at Ali and asked her the same question, and she made the same reply, though she went rather pink.

Pekka turned to Matti. 'You know,' he said, 'when I look at Dave I think that everything is all right. But when I look at Alison I think that everything is not all right.'

At last we admitted that we had a cash-flow problem, and a huge grin came over Pekka's face.

'You know what, brother? Today we get paid by our mission. We get paid in advance and they give us more because it's Christmas. How much do you want?'

We looked on in disbelief as he pulled out a bulging wallet and began to peel off notes. The two men insisted on loaning us enough money for us all to have a splendid Christmas, including the biggest Christmas tree we could find.

We had spent only six months in Austria when we heard that a major reorganisation was being planned. The British office of Open Doors was going to become independent from the rest of the work, for a variety of complicated financial reasons. The effect of this on us was that the work of the British office was going to be cut back: the Austrian base would be closed. Our old jobs in England had been filled by others, of course, so we had no jobs to go back to, either. In one swoop we found ourselves without a home, without a job, and without money.

We had a month to decide what to do, and at first we thought we would stay on in Austria. We had enjoyed our work among the Yugoslavs, in spite of the language problems: we spoke deplorable German and so did the

Yugoslavs, so on the whole we understood each other tolerably well! We looked to the Lord for guidance; once again, in our quiet times of Bible reading we waited for a verse to leap out and show us what we were to do. This time, however, the Lord indicated his will for us in other ways.

As we prayed about it, circumstances began to point the way: certain doors closed to us, while others opened. Our friends, Ieuan and Irene, wrote enthusiastically about a new house church that had started in Witney, and encouraged us to return home and help in building it up. And an Austrian pastor we knew gave us some good advice; we trusted his godly judgement and consulted him for his opinion.

'When I meet young people who speak fluent French,' he said with a twinkle in his eye, 'I advise them to do missionary work in France. Missionaries who speak good Spanish mostly go to Spain. I would suggest that people who speak English as well as you two do—well, maybe your mission field should be in England.' He must have realised that languages just weren't our strong point!

We decided to go back to Witney and once again the vexed question of accommodation arose. We had found it hard enough to find places to live while we were in the country, but doing so from abroad seemed almost impossible. We knew of only one vacant flat in the Witney area—a top floor flat at Cogges Priory, a parish just outside the town. I wrote to the rector, Howard Cole, and his wife Ruby, asking if we might use the flat until we found something more suitable.

Time went by but we had no reply. Then, six days before we were due to leave Austria, Ali went to the post office to pick up the mail. As she left with her arms full of letters she dropped one, and as she bent to pick it up she felt quite sure the Lord was saying to her, 'Ignore the contents of this letter.' She noticed that it was from Witney, and brought it back with the others.

When we opened it we found it was from Howard, reluctantly refusing our request; he had already written to the Diocesan Council to say that he would not be letting the flat again. Then Ali told me of her feeling in the post office.

I picked up Ali's guitar and went out on the balcony.

'Come on,' I said. 'We've done enough asking the Lord for the flat—now we're going to start thanking him for whatever it is he's doing about it!'

We started to sing our favourite Christian songs with enthusiasm, and got so carried away we almost drowned the sound of the phone ringing in the hall. It was Ieuan ringing from Witney. He told us he had just spoken to Howard, who told him an extraordinary story. Howard had been quite sure the flat was not to be re-let, but on the previous night his wife Ruby had a dream: she saw Jesus coming to her, and he said that on no account should they stop Ali and Dave having the flat.

Ruby, like her husband, had a real love for the Lord, and the dream was so real to her that she told it all to Howard. They agreed that we could live in the flat for three months, but no longer.

We were delighted to have a home in England once again; we assured them that we would leave their flat on the agreed date, even if it meant packing up without knowing where we were going. As things turned out, that was one assurance we were called upon to make good.

10

God's Provision

We now had somewhere to live, but I still needed to find suitable work. Open Doors had agreed to pay my salary for two months after we returned to England, so that we had a chance to settle down, but after that I supposed that I would just have to sign on the dole and draw unemployment benefit until I found a job.

However, as I prayed about our future, I became more and more uneasy in my mind about this plan. I came across a bookmark given to me by friends in Lymm, with a text on it: 'And my God will meet all your needs according to his glorious riches in Christ Jesus' (Phil 4:19). That's true, I thought, God is capable of supplying everything we need. But I pushed the thought away; I had a family to provide for, and it would surely be irresponsible of me not to make sure we had money coming in. The next day Alison was unpacking some books, and there was the bookmark again.

'Have you seen this?' she asked.

'Yes,' I replied. 'Several times. It seems to keep cropping up. I'm beginning to get the feeling that the Lord wants us to trust him for our income, not the DHSS.'

'That's good,' she replied, 'because I've had the same feeling.'

The more we prayed about it together, the more we felt sure that this was the right course of action, and we were intrigued to see how it would work out. One thing we agreed on was that we wouldn't tell anyone what we were doing, or drop big hints to people about our financial needs. That wasn't living by faith, it was playing on people's emotions.

The first day dawned when I didn't have a job, and I didn't have any money coming in either. As I got dressed that morning a thought darted through my mind: You're a fool—you've got no money now, have you? I wondered, Was that the Lord? No, it was accusing and spiteful, and I knew that it came from a different camp. Well, I thought, since the devil is the father of all lies, if I turn that round I could come up with the truth: I'm not a fool, and some money is coming in. So I started to thank the Lord for the provision he was going to bring our way, and went on down to breakfast.

Soon the post arrived, and the first letter I opened was from a friend in Cheshire whom I hadn't heard of in months. He hadn't been in touch with us, and knew nothing of our current situation. In his letter he said that he had been meaning to write for ages, but hadn't got around to it. However, he felt that he was being prompted by God to send us some money (something he had never done before) and he hoped we could find a use for it!

That cheque enabled us to live for the next few days; then other letters started arriving, enclosing gifts of money. Some of these were from friends who were living abroad, and certainly none of them knew of our financial difficulties.

At the end of that month I got a job as secretary to a surveyor in a building firm: then the gifts of money stopped arriving, as suddenly as they had started. I kept a careful note of what we had received that month, and wrote it all down in one column. Then I added up what we would have received in Social Security payments if I had signed on. When I saw what the figures were saying, I had to thank God for his goodness: our actual income had been twice what we would have received from Social Security. It proved to us once again that the Lord is a wonderful provider.

Meanwhile the time arrived when we had to leave the flat in Cogges Priory, and once again we were looking for accommodation. We packed all our belongings, wondering where we were to go, and trying hard to trust the Lord to provide a home for us. Just two days before we were due to leave, we had a visit from the wife of an RAF friend of Ali's brother. We didn't really know Maureen very well, but she was very concerned for us.

'We've been thinking,' she began. 'With Dave away all week, you could come and stay with us. It would be company for me, and the children are about the same age—they could play together.'

We didn't know what to say: Maureen scarcely knew us, but she was willing to have us share her house. We stayed with her for four months, before moving into Merryfield House, the headquarters of the Witney house church. Once again we were sharing—this time with two other families—and we learned a great deal about fitting in with other people in community life.

However, all this time we had been confined to one or two rooms, and we prayed hard and long for something more permanent to turn up. Although I was now working my income was still small, and with no savings buying a house was out of the question.

When we had been on the council's 'homeless' list for nearly a year, one of the elders of our church called to see us with some news. He had enough funds available to buy a house which we could rent: how soon could we move in? We were delighted to have somewhere to make a home of our own, and prepared to move immediately. There was one problem: we now had a whole house to furnish, with very limited resources—seventy pounds, to be exact.

It's amazing what you can do if you trust God. We went to auctions and found some incredible bargains—I'm quite sure the Lord must sometimes have closed people's eyes to the things we needed. Up until then all our accommodation had been furnished and the only thing we owned was a coffee table!

We found all our furniture in this way, but we still needed a fridge and a cooker. On the day before we moved we still had no money, but we told the Lord what we needed and waited patiently to see what the day would bring. In fact the post that day brought three separate cheques: one was the superannuation contributions which Ali had cashed in; another was from Mum, who always seemed to be helping us in the right way at the right time; the third was from a lady in America whose daughter had stayed with us for a while.

When we totalled the amounts, they came to just the sum we needed for the fridge and cooker. The thing that fascinated and delighted us was God's timing: those cheques could have come through at any time, but they came on the very day they were needed.

With a friend who had a car I went down to the show-room to select a cooker, keeping a careful eye on the price tickets. We finally selected one, and I asked if we could just pay for it and load it into the car.

'Oh, no,' replied the saleswoman. 'We don't supply cookers from here. You have to choose it here and then order it from the depot—it usually takes a week or ten days for delivery.'

'But that's far too long,' I said, my heart sinking, 'we're moving in tomorrow.'

'I'm sorry,' she said firmly. 'We don't supply cookers.'

I walked out of the shop, not knowing what to do, and John and I sat in the car and prayed. It was so frustrating: I had the money, and there was the showroom full of cookers, but there seemed to be no way that we could actually buy one and take it away.

On impulse, I went back into the shop.

'Is there no way you ever sell cookers from this shop?' I asked the saleswoman.

She looked up, rather surprised to see me back again.

'Well, no,' she said, a little less firmly this time. 'Unless they are shop-soiled...then we're allowed to.'

'Oh, I see,' I replied, pleased to have found a loop-hole in the system. 'Thanks.'

I went back to the cooker I'd chosen earlier, and examined it closely. It was in perfect condition, no marks or scratches or anything. It did need dusting, though—there was a thin film of dust over the surface.

'Er...' I hesitated. 'Look at this dust here—would you call that shop-soiled?'

Without the trace of a smile on her face she said at once, 'Yes, I would. Do you want to buy it?' And she went to the counter to write out the bill.

I joined her and began to write a cheque, but I had one final surprise in store. She saw what I was doing and stopped me.

'You're writing the cheque for the wrong amount—we give a ten per cent discount on shop-soiled goods!'

I was delighted with our purchases, and on the way home in the car I pondered on how the Lord provided for us. Why is it that the Lord apparently blesses some people and doesn't seem to favour others?

I firmly believe that the Lord has no favourites—we are all special in his eyes. He has laid down ground rules for the human race, and if they are followed, blessing will follow.

Further, I believe that whatever you sow, you will ultimately reap. If you sow corn, you reap corn; if you sow potatoes you reap potatoes. If you sow happiness into people's lives you'll get it back; but if the seed is bitterness that is what returns to you.

If you give your money freely, then it will return to you multiplied—but your motives must be pure. If your aim in giving is simply to enrich yourself, then the Lord will deal with that in his own way. But giving to God does work, and I found it out quite by accident on the first day I became a Christian.

It was the last meeting I attended at Filey that year, and at the end a collection was held in aid of foreign missionaries. Some were in great need, and we were encouraged to give what we could. I put my hands in my pockets to see what cash I had—in one pocket I had half a crown, and in the other a ten-shilling note. There was no doubt in my mind which I was going to give, and I held the half-crown in my hand ready to drop it into the bag!

But while I waited for the offering to reach me, I felt mean. I rehearsed all the reasons why I shouldn't give so much—I might need to buy something on the way home, I didn't know how the money would be spent on the missions, and so on. They all sounded pretty weak. Nowadays I would recognise the signs—it was the Lord telling me that this wasn't the amount of money he had in mind! When the bag came round I found myself giving the ten-shilling note and dropping the half-crown back in my pocket.

I thought no more about the incident until some time after I got home from Filey and had patched things up with my Dad. One afternoon Dad came up to me and said, 'Son, I want you to take this. I can see that holiday made a big difference to you and I want to contribute to it.' He pushed some money into my hands, and when I looked down I realised it was a ten-pound note. I had reluctantly given the Lord ten shillings and he had given me back ten pounds.

It was soon after that I was shown the principle of tithing, that is, giving one tenth—or more—of one's income and living on the rest. It's a sort of self-imposed income tax payable to God, only the difference is that he seems able to stretch the remainder of the income, so you often end up better off than when you don't tithe. You can read what the Bible has to say on the subject by looking at Genesis 28:22 and Proverbs 3:9.

I recall one time when things went badly wrong for us financially: the bills were coming in faster than the money and I decided to 'forget' to tithe that month—just until things got better. The next month was worse, and for the first time since our marriage we seemed to be swallowed up in debts.

Ali was confused, not knowing that I hadn't tithed our income the month before.

'Dave, I just can't understand this,' she said plaintively. 'The Lord's always been so faithful in the past. Why have we suddenly got all these bills?'

Sheepishly I admitted what I'd done—or not done.

'Dave, you idiot,' she said. 'How could you be so stupid?'

She was right. It was stupid to break one of God's laws so blatantly. We have always found that if we allow God to put his hand into our pocket, so to speak, he in turn allows us to put our hands in his pocket. 'And,' as a friend of mine once pointed out, 'he's got much bigger pockets than you!'

I quickly paid the tithe that we 'owed' and things started to work out again.

The point seems to be that God is not a sort of one-armed bandit, where you'll hit the jackpot if you press the right buttons. He has promised to provide for all our needs—but not necessarily all our wants, and sometimes there can be a world of difference between the two. There are many things I want that I don't need, but there is nothing I need that I don't have.

I have heard some people say that they can't afford to tithe. We're the opposite—we can't afford not to! It's sad that anything can be done initially out of a desire to please God, but may end up as a legalistic ritual. When a husband kisses his wife goodbye in the morning he does so not because he should, but because he wants to: the same principle applies to the commands of God.

I could write at length about the varied ways in which the Lord has supplied all our needs, but it would mean betraying the confidence of many people who just wanted to bless us, not find themselves in a book! And to give a balanced picture I would have to enumerate our own giving, which again should remain private. Believe me, though—tithing does work, and God is no man's debtor.

11

Wall of Fire

I remember when I was still quite small we went on one of our rare trips to the seaside. After a lovely day we returned home to find a problem: neither of my parents had taken a door key. I suppose they had both been so eager to leave the house that morning before the phone could ring and keep Dad at home, that they hadn't checked; each had assumed that the other would have one. As I stood on the front lawn with the others, the darkness surrounding us, I wondered how on earth we were going to get in.

I need not have worried. Dad was a policeman, and he knew a thing or two about housebreaking; in no time he had borrowed a ladder from Mr Renshaw's yard next door, found an insecure window, and climbed in. Soon we saw lights coming on inside the house and Dad opened the front door, and we realised we wouldn't be spending the night on the lawn!

Not a very remarkable story, but I give it as an illustration of the role of a dad. His children were stranded and vulnerable, and he was able to do something we couldn't do: get us into a place of safety. This world is full of dangers, and there are potential threats to our health and safety every minute of the day. Some are caused by our own thoughtlessness and stupidity, others are natural disasters over which we have no control. As I look back I am constantly aware of God's hand on my life: even on the day of my birth he chose that I should live rather than die with my twin. And as time has gone on I have been amazed and humbled to see how the Lord has stepped in and helped this clumsy, awkward child of his.

When Ali, Daniel and I were living in Austria, the Lord more than once showed his protective hand towards us. We lived in a large house on the edge of a village: the whole house was heated by an oil-fired boiler situated in the hall, next to a shower room. All the living accommodation, apart from one guest bedroom, was on the first floor.

We were assured that the oil in the tank would be sufficient to last the whole winter, but advised to check the level regularly, since it was necessary to order oil in advance, and delivery took several weeks. At the time, struggling with a new language, a new job and a new baby, we thought this seemed to be the least of our problems.

One night after a particularly busy day I found it difficult to sleep, and rather than keep Ali awake I decided to go to the living room and pray for a while. With so much that was new in our lives I had plenty to pray about, but that night, however long I spent in prayer, I still had a feeling that the Lord had something to say to me on a subject I hadn't touched on.

I asked God to show me what it could be, whatever it was that I needed to seek his guidance for, but I felt that there was no reply. In the end, in frustration, I said aloud, 'Well, if you're not going to tell me, I'm going to bed!'

Feeling better after my outburst I made for the door, but was stopped in my tracks by what seemed like a voice—not an audible voice, but words came into my head nevertheless.

'Go and check the boiler.'

This was silly, as I'd checked it only a few days earlier. However, again I had a deep impression just like a voice, saying, 'Go and check the boiler.'

I didn't much want to go downstairs in the cold in my dressing gown, but rather than go to bed with a niggling doubt I thought I had better obey—I knew the thing would be all right anyway.

When I got to the boiler room, though, I stopped thinking the whole exercise was a waste of time: the gauge was registering zero. I went back to bed feeling very solemn, and when Ali woke and asked what the trouble was, I told her we had a big problem on our hands. We were likely to be stranded without heating in the depths of an Austrian winter with a small baby to look after.

We prayed on the spot, asking the Lord to forgive us for not paying more attention to something so important, and asking for his help. We remembered the story in Exodus 15 where the children of Israel discovered water in the wilderness. When they found that the water was bitter, Moses put a piece of wood into it and it became sweet. In this bitter and dangerous situation we turned to the cross of Jesus, and asked him to turn it into good.

The next day I rang the British office of Open Doors and asked them to send us some money to pay for the oil. I made a wild guess at the amount: about £156. Then, rather than attempt a complicated telephone conversation in my shaky German, we decided to drive to the oil depot and explain our predicament in person. After our prayer in the dead of night we felt confident that the Lord would work something out for us.

The two young women in the office at the depot were very helpful. Yes, they agreed, they could have some oil delivered to us—would tomorrow do? I thought I had misunderstood them at first, but no, they really could deliver the next day. The Lord had one other mercy in store for us: although we were well into winter, this was the final week when we could buy oil at summer prices. Translated into pounds, the cost came to exactly the sum I had suggested to the British office—£156.

We went back to our car rejoicing, and thanked the Lord for his intervention. Now we could be safe and warm all winter.

We were thankful that the Lord had alerted us to that danger, in spite of our carelessness and lack of attention to detail.

There was an amusing sequel to this. When we got in the car I found that I had left my sunglasses in the office, so back I went, only to find that the staff were having their lunch break. I rapped on the window and one of the women came to the door with a sandwich in her hand. I tried to explain what had happened, but got my German mixed up: instead of *vergessen*, which means 'forgotten' I said *gegessen*, which means 'eaten'. What I actually said was, 'Excuse me, but I think I have eaten my sunglasses!'

We left the office with the sunglasses, as the two women stared at this strange Englishman with the peculiar eating habits!

There was another incident that occurred in Austria, however, which might have had even more serious repercussions without the Lord's help.

The shower room in our Austrian house was downstairs, near the guest bedroom. It was a large room, about twenty feet long, with a washing machine on the right-hand wall, and the shower at the end of the room on the left. There was no shower curtain, but a fairly deep base to step down into, and separate taps for hot and cold water.

Each morning I would start the day with a lovely hot shower, usually to the accompaniment of a tape of Christian music playing on my portable cassette player. On this particular morning I put the tape player on the washing machine and set it going loudly. Then I turned on both shower taps, adjusting them to the right temperature, and got in carefully. Everything went well until I had finished. The trick was to turn off both taps simultaneously; otherwise you would be forced to finish with a freezing cold shower, or worse, scalded by the almost boiling water coming from the hot tap alone.

As I turned off the taps the unthinkable happened. The cold tap turned off at once, but the hot tap refused to move! I immediately tried to turn the cold water on again, but my hands were wet and slippery and I couldn't move that one either. The whole thing happened very fast, and I knew that if I didn't move out of the shower immediately masses of scalding water would come cascading down on my naked body. Yet I was quite unable to move quickly: my disabled leg meant that I had to climb very slowly and carefully in or out of the deep shower base.

It was no use shouting for help: Ali was upstairs, and would never hear me above the noise of the tape and the washing machine. In any case, she could not reach me in time to help. Instinctively I just shouted out,

'Jesus, help!'

Then the most incredible thing occurred. One minute I was in the shower, aware of the scalding water beginning to hit my body; the next moment I was lying at the other end of the room, near the door, watching the nearly boiling water stream down an empty shower! I still have no idea how I got there, no recollection of being lifted or carried or anything. All I know is that I didn't get out of the shower by my own efforts, and however I arrived at the other end of the room, naked and dripping wet, I was not at all bruised or hurt by my sudden and dramatic transport. I was aware that God had broken into my life again—breaking the rules if you like—in order to save me from what would have been a severe scalding.

When you have experienced things of this nature, it gives you tremendous hope in other difficult situations. Always at the back of my mind I am aware that God is a loving and caring Father, with the power to move dramatically in our lives. It underlies the way I deal with my concerns about my family, especially Terry. On several occasions when we have prayed about Terry, the Lord has directed our thoughts to Psalm 91:15. 'He will call upon me, and I will answer him; I will be with him in trouble, I will deliver him and honour him.'

In Terry's situation our faith ultimately is not in what the government can do, nor in the actions of individuals, however well informed or well intentioned. I know that God can intervene in the ways of men. Just as he sent an angel to rescue Peter, he can intervene to save Terry—if that is within his plan. But whatever happens, we know that Terry is in God's hands.

Of course, it isn't always easy to see the way ahead, and at those times it can be hard to go on trusting; we have had experience of this, too.

One day during our time in Austria we visited some Russian friends of ours, who lived on the far side of a range of steep hills. When we set off for home after a very happy day, the sky was a deep midnight blue, spangled with thousands of bright stars. We admired the beauty as we wound our way up the hillside. As we paused on the summit, we were suddenly engulfed in a thick fog, and the valley below disappeared from view.

Along all Austrian roads there are tall poles every few yards, so that when the snows come, the road is still marked, and travellers can safely follow a path without fear of slipping over a precipice. However, on this occasion, the fog was so thick that we could not see the next pole until we had left the previous one behind. If we stayed at any pole, the car headlights could not pick up the next marker. A safe route was marked out for us, but we had to keep setting out in faith to follow it.

I believe that the Lord gives us markers on the road of our Christian lives too. Sometimes the marker is a word of scripture, just when you need to read it; a gift of money from a friend or stranger which comes just at the right time; or a friendly smile or word of encouragement when you are feeling down.

Look out for God's markers—I'm sure he is wanting to encourage you with them. Sometimes we have to be prepared to leave one situation without knowing what lies ahead; often then the future opens up in a way we would not have thought possible. Though the way seems slow and laboured, when we put our lives in God's hands he will eventually bring us out of the fog into a new and deeper security in himself.

Even after I had learned to trust God to care for me, I found I had to learn all over again to trust his love for my family. Daniel, our first son, had been a contented baby, enjoying perfect health, but his brother Michael had a more difficult time. We were living in Witney when Michael was born, and when he was only seven months old he caught measles and was very ill for a while. Even after he had recovered, he continued to have feeding problems.

By this time we had been home from Austria for about two years, and I had begun to speak at house church meetings; I had also experienced some healing and words of knowledge. On one particular evening the Lord gave me several words of knowledge. One by one they were acknowledged, but curiously, never directly. Everyone who claimed healing that night did so for a close relative or friend, not present at the meeting, who suffered from the ailments I mentioned.

When I got back home I recounted the evening's events to Alison.

'Every word was acknowledged, except one,' I told her. This seemed odd, because usually when people felt hesitant about acknowledging something in a meeting, they would come to me afterwards for private prayer.

'So which one were you left with?' asked Alison. She was lying in bed looking exhausted after an evening caring for Michael.

'The Lord showed me there was someone who had difficulty taking food, and difficulty keeping it down,' I said. 'I still feel it was from the Lord and that someone should have acknowledged it.'

'Dave,' said Alison, looking at me with her eyes filled with tears, 'don't you realise—you've just described Michael's problem exactly!'

She was right; at every feed Michael would bring up at least half the meal, and Alison would often have to change herself as well as him.

'Let's go and pray for him,' she said excitedly.

'What, now?' I asked. 'You said yourself he's only been asleep for half an hour.'

'I don't care if he wakes up,' she replied. 'I just want him to get better. I'm so fed up with him being sick all the time.'

Ali got out of bed and we went to Michael's room, where he was sleeping in his cot. We prayed for him and asked the Lord to heal him. As I laid my hand on his head he woke and started to cry—a cry we both recognised. He was hungry again!

'Right,' said Alison as she scooped him out of his cot, with a determined look in her eyes, 'he's coming with me. If he's healed I want to know, and there's only one way to find out.'

109

I followed her downstairs and watched in some anxiety as she put two Weetabix in a bowl and started to mix them with milk.

'Even on a good day, when other foods will stay down for a while, Weetabix never will,' she said, stirring away. 'So I suppose you could call this the ultimate test.'

She finished mixing the feed and began spooning it into Michael. I wanted to go and get a towel or something to mop up the resulting mess, but I didn't—and it would have been a waste of time. Michael wasn't sick that night, nor the following morning, nor since! He has grown into a sturdy boy with a very healthy appetite—and even through the usual childhood illnesses he is hardly ever sick.

We were immensely relieved and grateful to the Lord. And I was very amused when I realised how reluctant I had been to claim that word of knowledge for my own family. Yet how could God love my children less than I do? All my intense human fatherly love for my children is only a shadow of the love of the one who created us.

There was a similarly dramatic event concerning Daniel at about the same time. We had gone to stay with Ali's parents in Purley, and on one grey day Daniel and I set off alone to indulge Dan's great passion—train spotting. I was resigned to a cold morning on the platform at East Croydon, but Daniel had other ideas. He badgered me to buy tickets for a short train ride, and in the end I gave in.

However, I suddenly began to feel anxious, for no apparent reason. I asked the Lord why I felt so disturbed, but only felt him urging me to pray—but I didn't know for what.

I have often found that when I have difficulty coming up with the right words for prayer, the gift of tongues is a wonderful thing. It means that you can pray in the Spirit and know that you are speaking to the Lord, without having to think about every word. So I found myself battling away in tongues without knowing why. I soon found out.

We sat waiting for our train to come in, watching other trains pull in, disgorge their passengers and take on more, and the guard walking along closing doors. At last our train arrived and I let Daniel climb on, while I collected our belongings from the seat. When I turned round I saw to my horror that the train was already beginning to move out of the station, with some doors still standing open, and no guard in sight.

I tried to shout for help but no sound came, and the platform was deserted anyway. The train was gaining speed and on impulse I started sprinting after it.

Now anyone who knows me knows that I don't sprint anywhere! The Lord had touched my body on at least two separate occasions but as I still walk with a limp I find it difficult to move quickly. Yet the next thing I knew I was running alongside the train and actually overtaking compartments; I felt a tremendous surge of power in my body. The door of Daniel's compartment was still open, and I suddenly found myself being flung headlong through it (I could never have climbed in by myself—I find it difficult enough when a train is stationary).

Daniel was absorbed in looking out of the other window, and oblivious to the whole thing. When he heard me arrive with a crash he turned round, and said,

'Gosh, Daddy, you did get on the train fast, didn't you?'

I sat silent for a few minutes, recovering, and thanking the Lord. Once again he had intervened in my life and saved my child from a dangerous and frightening situation—by enabling me, for a fleeting moment, to run faster than I had ever run in my life before!

It gives me the greatest possible sense of security to know that God's fatherly love is caring for my family. In the book of Zechariah the Lord was speaking to the prophet about future events, and said, 'Run, tell that young man, "Jerusalem will be a city without walls because of the great number of men and livestock in it. And I myself will be a wall of fire around it," declares the Lord, "and I will be its glory within" ' (Zech 2:4,5).

Often as I look back over my life, I have felt that I have indeed been surrounded by a wall of fire. God in his love has protected me from events and situations that have been bigger than I could cope with—just as any loving father would.

12

One Step at a Time

Alison and I were glad we had decided to settle in Witney; we enjoyed living there and we found a close fellowship in the house church. I had a job as manager of a decorating shop and we were happy living in our own little house. The rest of the family were well, too: my mother was still living in Cheshire, and as busy as ever with her various activities. Diana had married and was living near her, and Terry and his family had returned to England and were settled in London. Terry's years overseas meant that he had built up an extensive network of contacts all over the world, and when the Archbishop of Canterbury wished to appoint an envoy to represent the Church of England abroad, Terry was the obvious choice. My mother was delighted to have the family within reach once again.

Meanwhile Alison and I had presented her with two more grandchildren: our daughter Caroline was born in 1980 and baby Matthew three years later. It looked as though we had all settled down for good.

However, Alison and I had finally come to a difficult decision: we were going to leave the house church. I suppose a church is like a river—it expands and grows and changes direction as it meets with other streams and water-ways. So we found that the church we attended grew and changed direction, and increasingly we found it was not a direction we could flow with. Realising this was a painful experience, and when we finally stopped attending, it was like a bereavement or divorce. We had happy memories of the past, but sadly by the time we left we felt so bruised and scarred emotionally that we didn't want to join another church immediately. We needed a breathing space, and for a while we worshipped together at home. During that time our own faith and relationship with the Lord was still strong—but we needed to know where our own spiritual home was to be.

One dull Sunday afternoon in winter we were all enjoying a quiet day at home. The living room was warm and cosy, and I was holding Matthew in my arms and watching him chuckle and gurgle. I was just thinking how good it was that none of us had to go out on such a cold day, when a thought seemed to come into my head from nowhere: the Lord wanted me to go to the local Elim Church that evening. I was intrigued—we hadn't attended any place of worship for the last few months, and this was the last thing I expected.

Mentally I began to debate this idea. The Lord couldn't really want me to go out this evening. I hadn't had my tea, I knew hardly anyone there, and I didn't want to go on my own. I must have imagined the whole thing.

However, the Lord didn't intend me to get out of it that easily. The next thought I had—and by now it was rather like a silent argument between me and God—was even more surprising.

'Not only do I want you to go out tonight, I want you to take Daniel with you.'

Now this I knew was silly. Daniel had given his heart to the Lord at a very early age, but like us he had found the going tough towards the end of our time at our last church, and he was heartily relieved that we were not attending church on a regular basis. I knew he wouldn't want to come with me.

Sure enough, the Lord replied to this effort. 'He will,' came the assurance. 'Ask him.'

Daniel was sitting on the floor looking at a book, and completely unaware of my silent conversation with God. He looked up in surprise when I spoke to him.

'Dan, I'm thinking of going to the Elim Church this evening. Do you want to come along?'

'Oh, yes, please, Dad,' said Daniel immediately, much to my astonishment. 'What time do we have to leave?'

Ali prepared an early tea for us, and we went along that first evening feeling very strange. We were received, of course, with a warm welcome, and soon the whole family was attending regularly. The numbers at the church were never large, and we all felt accepted and loved in that small community. Ali and I became members, and eventually I was appointed as one of the Elders. Ali played the piano at the Sunday meetings, I took occasional services, and a Bible study and prayer meeting was held in our home. We learned a great deal, and we all felt that we were growing in the knowledge and love of the Lord.

Eventually, though, after five years, we felt that it was time to move on again. There were hardly any children in the church, and we could see that all our children were at a stage where they needed friends of their own age who shared their beliefs. We felt very torn when we realised that this was what God wanted us to do, but in the end a move was inevitable.

We had no idea where the Lord might want us to go, but Ali and I prayed about it independently, and we both felt that he was directing us to the Methodist Church in Witney. We started to attend on Easter Sunday 1988, and again we have found a warm and friendly fellowship where we feel very much at home. The services are different from those we have been used to in the past, but we both know that this is where the Lord wants us to be, and the children love the many things they can now be involved in.

Ever since we married, Ali and I have had a routine of praying together each morning, committing the day into the Lord's hands. Often we listen to a news bulletin on the radio first, and use that as a reminder of world events needing particular prayer; then we pray for each other's activities, and for the children's. We have always felt it to be very important to 'cover' each day in prayer, so that whatever happens, we can entrust it to God.

This long-standing routine was very useful when Terry disappeared, and every morning he and the rest of the family were added to our list. After all our many answers to prayer, we know this is not just an empty ritual; we know that the Lord hears our prayers, even when we do not see immediate results. Of course we have not been the only ones to pray for Terry: recently I spoke to Dr Billy Graham when he was visiting this country, and he assured me that millions of Americans are praying for Terry, and so are others all over the world.

One thing that has struck us is the interest and concern shown by so many children. Several schools have been in touch with Terry's wife Frances and with my mother, and we know quite a few families whose children pray regularly for Terry. I'm sure God honours the prayers of a child in a special way, and I'm equally sure that one day they will be answered.

Sleeping has been difficult for me since Terry disappeared. However much you know someone is in God's hands, and that he has the power to change situations at any time, one is still human, and I have not found sleep to come easily. I've also found myself to be under stress, getting irritated by little things before I realise what is happening. There seem to be no rules, no time limits on a situation like ours, and although it is enormously helpful to take all our problems to the Lord, still every day we have to face them afresh. Terry has been travelling abroad for many years now, and I am accustomed to his absence, so I was surprised that I reacted with so much concern to his disappearance—I suppose it proves how strong is the underlying bond between us.

Four things have strengthened me during the time that Terry has been away: the love and support of my own family; the care and concern of friends and other Christians; the daily reading of the Bible; and listening to music, especially Christian music. I often think back to the days long ago when only the rich could afford to pay minstrels to perform their music; in this electronic age we need only push a button to have music immediately, lifting our hearts and spirits.

If you have read this far you will realise that although I began to think about God at a very early age, it was not until many years later that I found him to be real in my own life. Since then, life has been an exciting adventure, and getting to know Jesus better has been a thrilling experience—far too good to keep to myself.

Possibly you, too, had never realised that there was something you had to do in order to become a Christian. Perhaps, like me, you were never told that just because you live in a 'Christian' country, that doesn't automatically make you a Christian, any more than living in a garage makes you a car!

I would like to outline for you how to come to know Jesus Christ personally. There is no neat formula that I can pass on that will immediately give you a relationship with Jesus: everyone comes to him in a different way. However, the Bible gives us guidelines which help us to accept Jesus as our Saviour.

First, you must understand that God loves you. No matter what you have done or what you have been through, the fact that God loves you remains true. In John 3:16 it says, 'For God loved the world so much that he gave his only Son so that anyone who believes in him shall not perish but have everlasting life' (Living Bible). Try reading that verse again, putting your own name where it says 'the world' and 'anyone'—make it personal.

Second, you must repent of your sins. To repent means to turn around and start to go in a different direction, to start walking in a new way. It's not just being sorry for what you have done, it's changing your habits and lifestyle if necessary. Jesus said, 'Unless you repent, you too will all perish' (Lk 13:3).

Third, you must receive him as your Saviour and Lord. Realise that you cannot save yourself, stop struggling and let him take control of your life. Accept God's offer of love and forgiveness. Trust Jesus completely. 'But as many as received him, to them gave he power to become the sons of God, even to them that believe on his name' (Jn 1:12, AV).

Fourth, you must confess Christ publicly. Jesus said, 'If anyone publicly acknowledges me as his friend, I will openly acknowledge him as my friend before my father in heaven' (Mt 10:32, Living Bible). The Bible also says, 'If you tell others with your own mouth that Jesus Christ is your Lord, and believe in your own heart that God has raised him from the dead, you will be saved' (Rom 10:9, Living Bible). I thought that I would be a secret Christian, in case I couldn't live up to God's standards, but if I had succeeded in keeping my faith a secret it would have faded and died. We need the love and support and encouragement of each other to live the Christian life to the full.

If what you have just read strikes a chord in your heart, and you want to make a committment to Christ, don't put it off, do it now. You may have every intention of doing something about it at a later date, but we are not promised tomorrow. One of my father's favourite sayings was, 'The road to hell is paved with good intentions.' Don't let becoming a Christian be a 'good intention' you never got round to.

Just tell God in your own words that you are sorry for the things that you have done that you know are wrong, that you want to repent of these things, and receive Jesus as your Saviour, and confess him as Lord of your life.

If you say that to God and really mean it, then the Bible tells us that you will become a member of Christ's Body, in whom Jesus lives. And don't let your feelings tell you differently; stand on the authority of Scripture.

Doesn't it make sense to hand your life over to the one who made the universe and everything in it? Who knows what tomorrow may bring? Just as a captain who is travelling in unknown waters hands over his ship to a pilot who knows the waterway well, so you can hand over your life to the one who knows all the secrets of tomorrow. He knows how to guide you through safely, and no problem is too large for God to handle. So why not give him a chance in your life?

What does the future hold for the Waite family? What will we be doing, where will we be going?

One night many years ago, Alison and I both woke unexpectedly in the middle of the night. We couldn't explain it, but we were both suddenly aware of the presence of God, and we wanted to pray together. This need for prayer was so urgent that we prayed in tongues, not knowing what the Lord wanted to tell us. Afterwards I started speaking out what I felt: it was as though God was saying,

'Don't be surprised when this or that happens, when I take you here or there.' He shared many things with us that night; some of them we have seen happen, others are yet to come about. But whatever the Lord does with us, wherever he takes us, this we know—we will be walking with him. One step at a time.

A Time For Heroes

by Brother Andrew

Today is a time for heroes.

But the battle is not a glamorous one. 'Most heroes of the faith in the Bible become martyrs. One big problem in our time is that our heroes of the faith are celebrities.'

Looking at nine Bible characters, Brother Andrew shows how God calls his people to be warriors. All he looks for is our willingness to open up to him. And the wonder is that, as we do this, he gradually transforms us into men and women who shape history.

'Brother Andrew describes vividly the spiritual battle raging all over the world and offers us training to be heroes who will put our lives on the line and thus win the war.' —Josef Ton, President, Romanian Missionary Society

BROTHER ANDREW, known to millions as 'God's Smuggler', is founder and International President of Open Doors, a missionary organisation helping the suffering church worldwide.

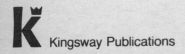

Kingsway Publications

Set Them Free

by Lida Vashchenko

A powerful story of suffering, faith and freedom.

Lida Vashchenko was a key figure in the Siberian Seven, a group of Pentecostals trapped for five years in the American Embassy in Moscow. What drove her there?

Raised in Siberia, forcibly removed from her home as a child because her parents were Christians, Lida's story is one of deep faith forged in the furnace of persecution.

Set Them Free tells the story of her years in an orphanage, where communist authorities tried to convince her to renounce her faith; the systematic persecution of her family; the heartbreaking story of her adopted son, Aaron; and the dramatic details of her escape to freedom. Gradually but forcefully the picture emerges of a young woman willing to pay any price for the sake of her remaining faithful to Christ.

Lida now lives in California, and is married to fellow exile George Gergis. They have one son, Jeremiah. Lida is actively involved in helping Christians in Russia, especially through her organisation 'Set Them Free'.

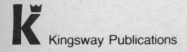

Kingsway Publications